REMEMBERING
WHY WE
PREACH

"The West African term *sankofa* means 'Go back and fetch it.' It conveys the understanding that we cannot go forth until we know from whence we've come. While Bellinger and Connors don't use this term, they do encourage Christian preachers to go back and fetch what is absolutely essential before going forth to preach. *Remembering Why We Preach* reminds us that the power of preaching lies not in the preacher but in the person of Christ—a person we may encounter most intimately in the form of a retreat. Bellinger and Connors astutely draw upon the deep well of preaching tradition honed over their years of teaching about preaching. This is not just a book about preaching; it is also an invaluable resource for preachers to which they may go back often before going forth to proclaim the Gospel!"

Deacon Melvin R. Tardy Jr.
President of the National Black Catholic Clergy Caucus

"Preaching *must* improve. But how? This retreat workbook is valuable precisely because it meets this urgent need—the *how* of better preaching—making years of homiletic wisdom available to a wide audience. May this book bear much fruit!"

Fr. Joshua J. Whitfield
Author of *The Crisis of Bad Preaching*

"Bellinger and Connors challenge good preachers to become better preachers by going deeper into their own prayer practices and deeper into living and preaching the Paschal Mystery. Offering a rich bibliography of preaching samples and resources in combination with a set of personal reflective exercises, this book promises to keep preachers moving deeper into their vocation for years to come and promises to strengthen the power of Christian witness to our world."

Ann M. Garrido
Associate Professor of Homiletics
Aquinas Institute of Theology

"Taking a community-oriented multimedia approach to homiletics, *Remembering Why We Preach* is a comprehensive exploration of the human, spiritual, pastoral, and practical aspects of the homily. An indispensable real-world resource for all in the ministry of preaching."

Deacon Brian Conroy
Director of Deacon Formation
Archdiocese of Los Angeles

"What a generous gift! This book offers years of scholarship, teaching, training, coaching, mentoring, and prayer shared in a practical, accessible, and layered format. Preachers, be generous. Go deep with this guide on your own or, even better, with a group. The Church will be grateful."

Rev. Kenneth Simpson
Vicar for Professional and Pastoral Development of Priests
Archdiocese of Chicago

"I have been preaching for more than fifty years and find this book stimulating, informative, encouraging, and filled with excellent suggestions and wonderful resources to help me further improve the special vocation of preaching. This unique resource is flexible and easily adapted for individuals, small gatherings, or larger study groups. Bellinger and Connors have written an excellent guide with informative text and spiritually rich retreat features that will help new and veteran preachers alike to keep always before them *why*, *whom*, and *to whom* we preach."

Bishop Paul J. Bradley
Diocese of Kalamazoo

A RETREAT
TO RENEW
YOUR SPIRIT AND SKILL

REMEMBERING
WHY WE
PREACH

Karla J. Bellinger AND
Michael E. Connors, CSC

Ave Maria Press AVE Notre Dame, Indiana

Scripture texts in this work are taken from the *New American Bible, revised edition* © 2010, 1991, 1986, 1970 Confraternity of Christian Doctrine, Washington, DC, and are used by permission of the copyright owner. All Rights Reserved. No part of the *New American Bible* may be reproduced in any form without permission in writing from the copyright owner.

———————————————————————

© 2022 by John S. Marten Program in Homiletics and Liturgics

All rights reserved. No part of this book may be used or reproduced in any manner whatsoever, except in the case of reprints in the context of reviews, without written permission from Ave Maria Press®, Inc., P.O. Box 428, Notre Dame, IN 46556, 1-800-282-1865.

Founded in 1865, Ave Maria Press is a ministry of the United States Province of Holy Cross.

www.avemariapress.com

Paperback: ISBN-13 978-1-64680-181-7

E-book: ISBN-13 978-1-64680-182-4

Cover image © gettyimages.com.

Cover and text design by Katherine Robinson.

Printed and bound in the United States of America is available.

Dedicated to

Fr. William Toohey, CSC,

the first homiletics instructor at the University of Notre Dame

and the director of campus ministry from 1970 until his death in 1980,

a social activist and much beloved preacher;

and to Virginia Armstrong Marten (1925–2022),

our beloved friend and gracious benefactor.

Contents

Introduction

Welcome to this retreat for preachers! Our goal here is to lead you through a renewal process so you will be better equipped to lead your people to God through your preaching. In the first part of this book, we'll help you attend to your spiritual life as a preacher, and in the second part we'll tend to the renewal of your preaching itself.

Preaching renewal and spiritual renewal walk hand in hand. When spiritual life is shallow, preaching life remains superficial. But when you and I have our hearts set on fire with the love of God, that graced fervor gives us much to preach about. As our spiritual life deepens, our preaching also deepens: we talk about God, whom we have met, whom we know, and whom we love. This faithful witness of a man or a woman of God is at the heart of effective liturgical preaching.

There may be times when we who preach settle too cheaply—we may smile pleasantly in the back of church when a parishioner files past and says, "Nice homily, Deacon"; "Loved the homily, Father"; or "Thank you for the wonderful homily, Bishop." And there are also those profound moments when a person says sincerely, "Your homily really moved me. It brought me closer to God." "Your preaching made me see my life differently." Or, "You made me want to take my relationship with Jesus more seriously." Those moments of connection are rich and meaningful for both preacher and listener; it can feel as if this response is what we minister for—and when we are called to preach, it is! This is why we do what we do: we want to bring our people closer to God. God is at the heart of it all. Nothing else matters so much as that.

Go Deeper

Studies of people in the pews tell us that they want their preachers to go deeper.[1] They want to meet Jesus. They hunger for a richer indwelling of the Holy Spirit. They may not be able to explicitly articulate that longing, but they recognize that they are looking for God in the preaching.

We as preachers also want to go deeper. We want to bring our people into an encounter with God. Yet there is an invisible and unknowable element to "encounter" that is not ours to effect. The Holy Spirit is the one who is at work in the inner life of each person. You and I have no control over the conversion of someone else. But we *can* preach in a way that makes an encounter with the living God more likely to happen.

How does this happen? God has already spoken to our people in many (sometimes hidden and/or implicit) ways. In our preaching, we can explicitly name that sense of God being present. We can nurture the fruit of that ongoing interaction and can help them to fall more deeply in love with God. As spiritual leaders, we seek to form a faith community that is on fire with the love of Jesus. Our people will then "go out" to transform the world in which they live.

This is a high ideal. To reach that ideal, the central question for this retreat for preachers, then, is this: How can we as preachers be renewed, deepened, and strengthened so that our preaching leads our people toward an encounter with God? This question is the soul of what we will explore together. This question is at the very heart of the spiritual life of preaching. This question is at the core of our vocation as ministers of the Word.

How Can This Retreat Process Help You and Your Preaching?

As a preacher, you yourself have encountered God at some point in your life. You study scripture. You preach. You celebrate liturgy. You pray for your people. Just picking up this book indicates that you are intrigued about how to strengthen your homiletic abilities to go deeper, to help others grow closer to God and to grow deeper yourself. So how can this retreat process help you?

At the ground level, you can work through this book by yourself, as a solo retreatant. Each chapter offers you introductory material with reflection or discussion questions to think about. You will then find suggested readings or homily viewing to help expand on the introductory materials. Finally, "Try This" exercises will help stretch your homiletic skills. We hope that working through these eight chapters can be profitable to you as a preacher both spiritually and in growing your homiletic skills.

However, while these materials can be used for individual reflection, we believe your experience will be enriched if you can find conversation partners, either in person or online. Change and growth are challenging on one's own. It can be hard to stay motivated. It can be hard to hold yourself accountable to the process. Others can help you in important ways:

- as discussion partners for the written materials,
- as listeners who help you to accurately assess your homilies (see the evaluation form in appendix 2), and
- as companions who can give you feedback when you are trying something new.

If you cannot find a traveling partner on this retreat journey, keep a log or journal as an alternate form of accountability. Record what you try, how things work out, and your thoughts and responses to the various steps along the way.

Your experience can be further enriched by gathering a group of peers willing to work through this retreat process together, perhaps through a series of monthly meetings stretching over most of a year. The Lilly Endowment of Indianapolis created an initiative in 2013 titled "Strengthening Christian Preaching" to improve preaching through the support of peers; they found that those in ministry were greatly helped by the support of others who minister. These particular written materials arose from our Notre Dame initiative funded by Lilly, which was called the Notre Dame Preaching Academy. We worked with and listened to almost a hundred Catholic clergy in that initiative over the span of four years. One thing we learned is that a robustly invested peer learning group can create a long-lasting and very positive impact on a preacher's life and preaching.

If you want to form a peer learning group, whom might you ask to walk with you? Seek a diverse peer group—diversity fosters the richest growth process. Gather a multigenerational group of Catholic priests, deacons, and/or lay preachers. Bring together an ecumenical ministerial association representing various Christian denominations. Incorporate this retreat into an existing support group. The support of peers is not requisite for renewal, but it strengthens this retreat process to have that companionship and accountability. The ideal would be to find six to eight people who would commit to learning together, supporting each other, trying new ways of preaching, observing each other's homilies, and challenging each other to grow in preaching skills and the spiritual life.

Try New Things and Grow

There are eight chapters to spur your thought and experimentation. You will not just be learning ideas *about* preaching. You will grow from concrete practical experience: Growth in preaching is challenging, whether on your own or with a group. Try new things. Challenge yourself. Your exertions are for the faith of your people; they are worth your best efforts. Don't be surprised to find yourself sharing insights such as, "I tried this; it was a new thing for me, and I failed at it miserably." Or, "This is what worked for me. My people have been praying more as a result!"

Seek feedback. This can come from dialogue partners in your parish or from your peer group. Feedback comes in three varieties: affirmation, evaluation, and coaching. As you try new things, it is helpful to have *affirmation*: "I really liked the way you did that!" It might also be beneficial to hear an honest *evaluation*: "That didn't really work because . . ." *Coaching* makes suggestions based on objective evaluation: "This might help you to grow in this way: . . ." Let people know which of the three kinds of feedback you are seeking. As you encourage those around you to help you in your preaching, you can build a lifelong expectation for feedback that will be of great benefit to you. Preaching the Word of God is a relational event. It can be enhanced through the insights of others.

If you are meeting with a group of peers, there is a suggested meeting outline to follow in the appendix. Try it! Those who have been faithful to that outline have experienced a meaningful time when they have gathered together. First, check in with each other to see how each is doing. Discuss your reading and how your learning from this retreat process has affected the way you have preached during the past month. Then watch and evaluate homilies and pray for those preachers and their people. When you close, decide how your group will take ownership of the learning process during the coming month. What will you read and/or view, and what skills will you agree to work on as a group?

The Flow of the Retreat Process

What does this retreat process look like? This renewal process builds from a statement of the US Catholic bishops, "The preacher then has a formidable task: to speak from the scriptures . . . to a gathered congregation *in such a way that those assembled will be able to worship God in spirit and truth, and then go forth to love and serve the Lord.*"[2]

First, in chapters 1–4, we turn inward and look at our purpose as preachers, our preaching identity, and our spiritual roots. In other words, we seek to remember *why* we preach. Chapter 1 clarifies the fundamental purpose of preaching: encounter with the Lord. To speak credibly from the scriptures, in chapter 2 we will investigate *whom* we preach about—the one who is the core of our faith in the Paschal Mystery. In the third chapter, we'll look at preaching and homily preparation as a spiritual practice. Chapter 4, "Preaching as a Pastoral Practice," emphasizes that the homily is a two-way relationship, a give-and-take between preacher and hearer.

In the second part of the book, we turn outward. In chapter 5 we look at the way the preacher affects others: the leadership role of preaching turns toward understanding the pathways through which listeners hear. A discussion on creating a congregational conversation is in chapter 6. In the final two chapters, we focus on crafting messages that move our people toward discipleship and then turn outward to mission.

Preaching for encounter pairs evangelization and homiletics: together we seek to preach on Sunday so that our people are empowered to witness God's redeeming love to the world they inhabit on Monday and through all the week until they come together again in worship. Placing encounter with God at the center of our preaching is the charge we have; it is the *reason* we preach.

As we created this guide, we have hoped in our heart of hearts that this retreat process will kick off a lifelong desire to deepen your preaching life. There is enough background material included in this book for you to use it for many years to come. You can come back to it when your preaching life is feeling shallow, so you can dig deep into a well of fresh water. Going deeper in preaching is a lifelong process!

This book is meant to be used in conjunction with additional readings and/or online videos, together with reflection questions, for each chapter. After each chapter's "Read or View" heading, you will find a link to the online folder of additional materials and a quick list of the items for each chapter. These files may be downloaded free of charge for those who purchase this book. All materials in these supplemental files are used with permission. Here is the link for you to bookmark now: https://bit.ly/Remembering-WhyWePreach. Or use this code:

Alternatively, send an email to the Marten Program at martenpr@nd.edu and request the files.

Thank you for your passion for the preaching of the Holy Gospel. We pray for the Holy Spirit to make your spiritual life rich and your preaching fruitful, for both the faith of your people and the glory of God!

Dr. Karla J. Bellinger
Fr. Michael E. Connors, CSC
John S. Marten Program in Homiletics and Liturgics
University of Notre Dame

PART I

Go In!
A Spirituality of
PREACHING

1.

Help Them
Find God

An encounter with Jesus Christ is the foundation of
discipleship. The focus for this retreat process is to
strengthen our ability and our understanding of how
to preach for encounter.

A Fresh Start

Here we are at the beginning. You may have picked up this book hungry to grow in
your preaching. You may have picked up this book because it is required for a preaching
course or a diocesan continuing education program. You may be starting to gather with
a group of peers to build new relationships rooted in your shared vocation as preachers
a place for friendship and support, and an opportunity for mutual challenge, as well as
to pray for each other and your parishes. For whatever reason, welcome!

 In the first half of this book, you will go inward to look at your own preaching life.
But we won't stay looking inward. In the long run, the focus becomes other centered,
helping you ask, How can my preaching become a wellspring where my people learn
to deepen in their encounter with the Lord Jesus Christ?

 The living God is both the source and the goal of *Remembering Why We Preach*.
The Lord has touched our lives. We want others to share in that experience. We want
them to encounter the living God whom we preach. This encounter is the purpose of
our preaching.

Our Deepest Desires as Ministers of the Gospel

Several years ago, I (Karla) talked with an experienced preacher about how listeners listen to homilies. He said he once had a parish that had seemed unresponsive to his preaching. He wanted them to be receptive. He wanted them to be moved by the love of God as he had been moved by the love of God. He wanted them to be changed by what he said in the homily within the Sunday liturgy. But he didn't feel that was happening. Discouraged, he sent out a survey and asked his people to respond.

He was totally taken aback at their response. Time after time, his people told stories. One came from a wife who had been comforted after her husband's death by one of this priest's homilies. Another story came from a young man who had embraced hope when life seemed dark. A man found courage to do the moral thing in a challenging time at work. Although the priest had not heard any of this feedback before, his people's stories fed his innermost aspirations: to help them find God.

We want our people to form a relationship with Jesus Christ. We want them to embrace discipleship. We want them to respond to our mutual call to holiness. These are our deepest desires as ministers of the Gospel. The love of God has changed our lives, and we want others' lives to be touched as well. Our own growth, discipleship, and holiness began with that personal "encounter" with God. We do not walk alone in that encounter. All through history, the Holy Spirit has been with us and has worked in surprising ways in and through countless others.

Encountering the Saints

The Christian spiritual tradition is replete with instructive stories of encounter. A Pharisee named Saul was knocked to the ground by a bright light and a vision of the One whom he was persecuting. Coming home late one night from a party, a wealthy youth named Francis stood mute for half an hour in a dark street of Assisi, overcome by the grandeur of God. A widow named Monica wept every day for her son Augustine, and he was converted in a garden. Springing from those encounters, each of these saints was launched into a life of a relationship with God. Repeated encounters and growing relationship transformed them into vibrant disciples.

The saints are models for us. An initial encounter does not suffice; it is repeated encounters that build relationship. If a freshman on a college campus interacts with another student only once at the beginning of the school year, that meeting remains an isolated incident; it does not grow into a relationship. If a five-year-old meets a friend on the first day of kindergarten and those children play together every day at recess for the next six years, a solid friendship forms. This is also how it works with God: the grace of God moves within a parishioner; he or she hears and responds to that call; that person then wants to pray often and overflows with the goodness of God; and a relationship grows with the living God, bearing fruit in a life of holiness. That life of holiness is the call for all of the baptized. Holy people transform the world around them. Encounter, relationship, discipleship, and holiness—these all flow together. And they all begin with encounter. Just as the saints encountered God over and over again and thus built a relationship that bore fruit in mission, we desire the same for ourselves and for our people. We are to be the saints for today, the prophets and the evangelists of our day and age; that is our mission as the baptized. To foster that mission is our call as preachers. It is the *reason* we preach.

Preaching for Encounter

The encounter with God comes in many shapes and forms and circumstances. So then what does it mean to *preach* for encounter?

It is no accident that many of the great saints of our tradition were known as great preachers, confessors, and spiritual directors. They knew how to lead people to God. They knew how to inspire both faith and commitment in those who heard them. It started with the authentic witness of their own lives. Then they used images, stories, and forms of language that stirred people toward a relationship with the Most Holy.

At the same time, those who personally knew an encounter with God also struggled to put words to their experience. Teresa of Avila described *touches* from God and a flame burning within her heart. Augustine spoke of the Holy Spirit bubbling up within the believer. John of the Cross wrote poetically of the fragrance of God's love and the whisper of his breeze. Brother Lawrence of the Resurrection spoke of the cultivation of continual encounter as the practice of the presence of God. Thérèse of Lisieux, in her physical weakness, spoke of ecstatic joy. The apostle Paul described the gift of inner courage to press on in the race (1 Cor 9:24; 2 Tim 4:7).[1]

We, too, yearn for words. How do we outwardly express those indwelling mysteries of God? It is not easy to speak of the Holy. We pray for words that will open eyes anew. We hope to facilitate a change of worldview or attitude or behavior. We may hear accounts of how a thought hovered within a hearer's memory for weeks and then ignited a flash of insight. We want to spark those oft-repeated encounters—encounters that grow into a burning love for God. Can we do that? It happened *then* through the saints. Can it happen *now* through *us*?

We believe that God first comes to meet us, that our God is, by nature, Self-Revealer (*CCC*, 50–52). The Almighty is at work. The kingdom of God is among us. God is *here*. The hand of the Lord can also seemingly break in from out of nowhere. We may not know how, but suddenly a change of heart happens. We cannot control how the Holy Spirit moves within us, and certainly not within another person, but we can and must cultivate an attitude of expectation that the Holy Spirit will stir. We do not know how God inspires a mind or fires a will, but in faith, we believe God wants to encounter us. Encounter may feel totally out of our control as preachers. We begin with trust. We preach in faith that God wants to speak to our people through us.

Discerning the Movement of the Holy Spirit

So, what can we preachers do to foster encounter between God and his people? In our experience, we have seen there are specific elements that homiletically encourage an encounter with God. There are modes of delivery, forms of presentation, and tones of voice that touch the heart. There are certain kinds of images, stories, and forms of language that are more likely than others to spark the imagination and lead people toward the Holy One. There are ways of structuring words that lead people on a journey toward faith. There are ways of preaching that help to bring God close.

In our preaching, we can tap into deep and universal human hungers—for meaning, hope, transcendence, and deep intimacy with the Divine Lover. We can help those for whom we preach cross the chasm between their lives and the love of God, through the agency of the Holy Spirit. It is a high calling to help our people to encounter God. We have to be listening. For in all generations, in all geographies, even as cultures and peoples change, the Holy Spirit still wants to speak. What does the Lord want to say right here and right now? That calls for discernment—an integral element of effective preaching.

Homiletic discernment encourages us to deepen our sensitivity to the movement of God. Why does that matter in this preaching renewal process? If we believe God wants to speak, that means that we, as preachers, matter. Our words matter. The holiness of our spiritual lives matters. Our prayers for our people and for our preaching matter. We ask God to speak through our thoughts, feelings, memories, and imagination. What the Lord wants to say may not be what we initially thought to say. As we pray, "Thy will be done," our homilies may move in a different and/or surprising direction. *God* wants to speak through us. Through our embodied witness and through our words, we *can* facilitate the experience of God. It is possible. Through us, as preachers, the Divine

Lover *can* draw people close. That belief is at the foundation of this renewal process. That belief is at the core of this book.

What does homiletic discernment mean? As in all discernment, it means to identify the path where the Lord is leading. In the case of a homily, to discern means to be listening, both in preparation and in delivery, to discover what God wants to say to these people right here, right now, through this scripture and through you, their spiritual leader. It is the place where human need meets God's self-communication. To be an instrument of God is a high calling.

In this book we will look at how to discern the core of your message, how to structure the homily to pass on a faithful message in a fresh and creative way, and how to listen to the needs of the people to whom you preach so you can speak the word of the Lord to them on one particular day. Homiletic discernment is spiritual work and lies at the heart of becoming better preachers.

Our people plead, "Go deeper." The Holy Trinity—Father, Son, and Spirit—pleads, "Go deeper." To lead people into an encounter with God is not superficial work. We discern and preach the living God who is present and active. God is here. God is at work. That One who is present is the heart of our message. That One who is present is the agent of encounter, the One who makes encounter happen. In the next chapter, we'll look at that more deeply.

Discuss and Reflect

1. Think about your own repeated encounters with God. They may come through prayer and liturgy, within family and community, and through reading, music and other arts, the created world, and much more. How does your consistency in allowing yourself to be found by God make a difference in the strength of your relationship with God? What happens to that relationship when you slack off in those pathways to encounter?

2. When you are preparing to preach, think of how you discern your message. How can you tap into the hungers all of us share, a hunger for meaning and fulfillment, a yearning for hope, a sense of transcendence, a desire for deep intimacy with the Divine Lover? What is your discernment process?

3. Change is challenging. As you begin this process of renewing your preaching, look at making small and achievable goals: to read, to try something new, or to improve your homiletic skills. Look ahead to the "Try This" section and the "Read or View" suggestions. Which of those resonates with you as something that could help you to grow? Accountability helps change to happen. If you are on your own in this process, tell one other person what you are going to try to do. If you are working within a peer learning group, publicly commit your goal(s) to each other.

Try This!

1. *Choose your spiritual reading.* At the beginning of this preacher renewal process, pick out at least one book to read for spiritual insight.[2] This could be an old and well-worn favorite. This could be a book you have always wanted to read but have never made the time for. It doesn't have to be related to preaching, but it could be. Dedicate a particular time and place to spend with this author and book to nourish your own spiritual life over the course of this upcoming year.

2. *Ponder.* For this chapter, consider a few of the spiritual writers who have influenced and inspired you, now or when you were younger. What makes them "succeed" in bringing you to God? How do they say things? What images and phrases do they use? What do they say that resonates with your experience as you read and pray with them today?

3. *Incorporate spiritual elements into your homilies.* Next, identify a phrase, theme, or image from your favorite author or saint that could help ignite the spiritual growth of your hearers. Incorporate at least one of those spiritual phrases, themes, or images into each of your homilies.

Just for an example, if you were to pick Pope Francis's *Evangelii Gaudium* as your spiritual reading, below are some of the words and phrases that articulate "encounter" in that apostolic exhortation. Incorporate a few of those words or thoughts in your upcoming homilies in ways that tie in with the Lectionary readings.

Receive	Overflow	Touch	Fire	Receive
Join	Enlighten	Awaken	Living Water	Encourage
Heart-to-Heart Communication	Quality Time	Desire	Strengthen	Let Go
Hope	Trust	Receive	Alive and Ardent	Enthuse

Read or View

Read or view additional materials found in this companion folder: https://bit.ly/RememberingWhyWePreach or use this code:

The materials for this chapter include the following:

James Keating, "Contemplative Homiletics," *Seminary Journal* 16, no. 2 (2010): 63–69.

Links to two homilies, one by Fr. Michael Holman, SJ, and the other by Fr. Peter Cameron, OP.

Reflection questions for all of the above. All materials used with permission.

Additional Reading for Spiritual Growth

Bloom, Anthony. *Meditations: A Spiritual Journey though the Parables*. Denville, NJ: Dimension Books, 1971.

Brueggemann, Walter. *Praying the Psalms*. Winona, MN: St. Mary's Press, 1993.

Dubay, Thomas. *Fire Within*. San Francisco: Ignatius Press, 1989.

Egan, Harvey. *Christian Mysticism: The Future of a Tradition*. Eugene, OR: Wipf and Stock, 1984.

Francis of Assisi. *The Little Flowers of St. Francis*. New York: Doubleday, 1958.

Francis. Apostolic Exhortation *Evangelii Gaudium* (*The Joy of the Gospel*). Washington, DC: US Conference of Catholic Bishops, 2013.

Francis de Sales. *Introduction to the Devout Life*. New York: Image Books, 1972.

Ignatius of Loyola. *The Spiritual Exercises of St. Ignatius*. New York: Image Classics, 1964.

John of the Cross. *Selected Writings*. New York: Paulist Press, 1987.

Lawrence of the Resurrection. *The Practice of the Presence of God*. Orleans, MA: Paraclete Press, 1985.

Lossky, Vladimir. *The Mystical Theology of the Eastern Church*. Yonkers, NY: St. Vladimir's Seminary Press, 1976.

Martin, James. *The Jesuit Guide to (Almost) Everything: A Spirituality for Real Life*. New York: HarperCollins, 2010.

Nouwen, Henri. *In the Name of Jesus: Reflections on Christian Leadership*. New York: Crossroad, 1992.

Rahner, Karl. *The Great Church Year: The Best of Karl Rahner's Homilies, Sermons, and Meditations*. New York: Crossroad, 1999.

Rosage, David E. *Speak, Lord, Your Servant Is Listening*. Ann Arbor, MI: Servant Books, 1987.

Taylor, Barbara Brown. *The Preaching Life: Living Out Your Vocation*, 8th ed. New York: Cowley, 1993.

———. *When God Is Silent*. New York: Cowley, 1998.

Teilhard de Chardin, Pierre. *The Divine Milieu*. New York: Harper and Row, 1960.

Teresa of Avila. *Interior Castle*. Mineola, NY: Dover, 1946.

Thérèse of Lisieux. *Story of a Soul: The Autobiography of St. Thérèse of Lisieux*, 3rd ed. Washington, DC: ICS Publications, 1996.

Weil, Simone. *Waiting for God*. Translated by E. Craufurd. New York: Harper & Row, 1951.

2.

Preaching the Paschal Mystery

The death and resurrection of Jesus Christ is central to our faith. God gives us a Redeemer who lifts us from darkness to new life, in a myriad of ways and places. The proclamation of the Paschal Mystery is the heart of our liturgy; integral to that, the Paschal Mystery is the heart of our preaching.

We Have a Redeemer

Picture the people to whom you preach. They are gathered in the pews, sitting before you on a typical Sunday in your parish. You know them. You love them. A single mother corrals her two preschoolers into a pew: it took an hour to get their teeth brushed, clothes on, and shoes cleaned to get here. A middle-aged man has just lost his job: he kneels and bows his head, his shoulders slumped with worry. The faces of three teenagers are etched with grief and confusion: their fifty-year-old mother died of cancer two weeks ago. A young woman is weighed down by loneliness and anxiety; she looks to the liturgy for renewed purpose in life. You stand to preach. You have something to say that will lift these people out of their darkness. In your prayer for these people this past week, you have wrestled with what the scriptures have to offer to them. Since preaching for encounter is at the center of our preaching, *who* is it that will help these people through their trials? In preaching for encounter, we discern *what* to preach, but most important for the salvation of our people, we discern *whom* we preach.

In this chapter, we will focus on that Someone who is at the heart of preaching for encounter. In Christian faith, we believe that our Trinitarian God—Father, Son, and Holy Spirit—wills our good. We believe that a relationship with God makes a difference in how we live and flourish. We believe that God is active and present and wants to be close to us. "God" is not just an idea to be talked *about*, nor merely a literary character in an old book. The Holy Spirit is God at work *here, now*. Jesus Christ is our Redeemer, the Savior of the world, who lifts us out of darkness and despair. This is the Good News we preach!

This Good News may be the message that you and I live and breathe. We perhaps even take it for granted. But for us as well as for the people to whom we preach, many other "redeemers" are also offered: a double shot of espresso in a tall latté can lift us from exhaustion to energy; we can be transformed from despair to exhilaration through a last-minute "Hail Mary" finish at a football game; and we could climb Pike's Peak to rejuvenate our sagging spirits. These are all good things. These are all gifts from God. But redeemers? Created things cannot rescue us.

As a preacher, you are a spiritual leader. As their leader, you get to know your people. You know their joys. You know their sorrows. But the marketers for Starbucks® have also studied their joys and struggles. Advertisements for beer during a televised football game imply that a drink can lift fans to happiness. Self-help books and websites offer techniques and foods and exercises and identities and drinks and ways of thinking—these are all designed to move us toward betterment. So many saviors! So many options! American culture carries an implicit message that with the help of our product you can do what you want to do, it's all up to you! That jobless man in your pew is bombarded by messages to buy or believe in other redeemers. Which will he choose? Jesus Christ is only one among many options.

This secular bombardment may or may not be part of your own life experience. As you pray the daily office, you are immersed in the psalms, which call for the help of God. At daily Mass, you are surrounded by the message of the redemption of Jesus Christ. You may live and breathe the message of the salvation of the Son. So you may feel as though salvation and redemption are a part of all that you do and all that you talk about.

Here is the irony we have found from coaching Catholic preachers: although homilists think they talk about the grace/help/movement/agency of God all the time, when we have had them analyze their own preaching, they are surprised to discover they do not. The help of Jesus, the comfort and/or moving of the Spirit, the urging of the Father, the agency of God at work—we know this stuff so well! But strangely, it does not show up in the homily. The grace that is at the foundation of our faith? It remains implicit, unnamed, assumed, hidden—at least partially—in the background. Preachers assume they are conveying things they are not.

Words from the pulpit too often leave listeners to follow God of their own volition, on their own steam. We tell people, "Be better," and then we leave them to do that through our own efforts. This message is not all that different from what the secular world preaches. Pelagian preaching is more common than many preachers realize.

Let's look more closely at that. We believe in the Paschal Mystery of the One who lifts us from crucifixion to life. Yet that is not the daily experience of those who sit in our pews. The redemption of Jesus as the source of strength and flourishing—it is only one choice among many. For the sake of our people, we are compelled to more explicitly name the who of their salvation.

The Person of the Paschal Mystery

Christianity is not a self-help faith. Christian hope places its trust in the Divine Agent who wants to transforms us. Do our people know that? The ones in the inner circle whom you see at the parish most often—the daily Mass goers and the Bible study groups—yes, they probably do recognize "who" it is that changes us. Those are likely to be the ones you have the most interaction with, the ones who love you and give you the feedback of what a good homilist you are.

But what about the five out of six weekly attendees who are not involved in anything other than Sunday Mass? In a world that is so loud with other redeemers, we cannot assume that those people grasp the central Christian message; God is just one choice among many. Those who attend Mass irregularly or once a year are even further from the daily experience of redemption brought by a personal God. As we look at homiletics at its intersection with evangelization, we must acknowledge that our people are inundated with a multitude of redeemers.

Why does this matter? A few generations ago, it was expected in American culture for people to turn to God when they needed help. That cultural mindset is still common in Christian cultures of many countries, especially in the southern hemisphere: when you need help, you turn to God. But that is no longer the mainstream expectation in the United States, Canada, and Western Europe. For most of our people, there is no One, no Other, to whom to turn. Even many churchgoers are theological deists—God may be "out there" somewhere, but not really much involved, watching from a distance.[1] When there is no divine Other who is our foundation, rates of anxiety, depression, addiction, abuse, and suicide increase, especially among the young; they find their choices overwhelming and their own strength insufficient. They are bombarded by noise that proposes help from many places. And usually Jesus Christ is not one of those options.

Internalizing the Paschal Character of Christian Preaching

The proclamation of the Paschal Mystery is at the heart of our preaching, for the homily is integral to the liturgy, "Every homily, because it is an intrinsic part of the Sunday Eucharist, must therefore be about the dying and rising of Jesus Christ and his sacrificial passage through suffering to new and eternal life for us."[2] The homily is not an interlude or an interruption between parts of the Mass; rather, it is firmly embedded within the liturgy, as an essential part of Catholic worship.[3] The homily doesn't merely serve worship; it *is* worship. The fathers of the Second Vatican Council saw an important connection between the two movements of the Mass: "The two parts which, in a certain sense, go to make up the Mass, namely, the liturgy of the Word and the Eucharistic liturgy, are so closely connected with each other that they form but one single act of worship" (*Sacrosanctum Concilium* 56).

The eucharistic liturgy always celebrates the Paschal Mystery. Precisely here, Christians experience the most profound depths of God's love. The Crucifixion shows us how far Christ would go for us. The death of Jesus assures us that our sufferings, too, are noticed by God and have meaning. There is no suffering, no death experience, where Christ will not accompany us and ultimately rescue us. No sin or shortcoming can stand between us and the crucified Lord. The Resurrection gives us courage that new life lies beyond and through our sufferings, and that mercy trumps guilt. Death is not the final word. The tomb is empty.

As we speak those homiletic words of grace, we as preachers participate in the nearness, the transcendence, and the gracious action of the Divine Partner. Hear again that essential thought: *we as preachers participate and share in the agency, the action, of the Holy Spirit.* Our preaching matters. Our words matter. "Preaching exists in the Church to be a life-saving presence that reaches out to those in peril and that rescues them from their despair, their demise."[4] The task is urgent. The personal God is the source of conversion; at the same time, the Holy Spirit also dwells within us and works through us as preachers for the sake of the community's faith.

How Do We Preach the "Who"?

We need to preach a personal, available, here-and-now-present God. But how can we do that? Let's look at a few techniques for ensuring that our hearers meet the divine Person who is our reason for preaching.

Content

In our homiletic content, we can pass on the message that no, our own effort, our own strength, is not adequate to handle life's trials. We are not alone; the world as we see it is not all that there is. We can weave in an opening or a closing line or paragraph that says we believe the God who is Father, Son, and Holy Spirit *is real*. We can let the hungry hear that God desires to show himself to us within a rich, intimate, and passionate relationship. The *who* of our faith, the *agent* of redemption, is a person, and so our relationship to the agent of our redemption must be personal. It cannot remain an abstraction.

Structure

The way we structure our preaching often leaves out what God is doing. Many of the homilies we have analyzed follow this exegesis-application form:

1. Sometimes start with a joke or a story.
2. Unpack the scriptures, and name what it is that we believe.
3. Tell people how to live their lives; name what they should think and do and how to live out this message.

But something is missing! How do we get from: (2) belief to (3) action? Do we have to do it all by ourselves?

At the core of Christianity, we have Jesus Christ our Redeemer who brings us from death to life. The grace of God transforms our darkness into light and our despair into hope. God is our hope. Spend much time naming the here-and-now *action* of the Father, Son, and Holy Spirit in your preaching. Structure your homily around the task of showing your people the action of God who moves us from darkness to light and from hope to despair. Make this depiction of God an entire move within your homily. Often when it is mentioned, grace comes in only one sentence tacked onto the end of the homily: "May God help us to . . ."

Meet the Teacher

What happens in our preaching if we forget to highlight the activity of God, the agent of transformation? Our preaching remains superficial and shallow. The culture of individualism can seep into our preaching, making our message (semi-) Pelagian. If we do not mention the help of God, we implicitly preach that our own human agency is all that we need to live a good life, as though we can "make it" on our own. One listener implored for the homily to be more than something "just to make you feel good, which you can get at the Kiwanis Club or the Rotary Club or somewhere else."[5] We have to more robustly name *who* it is who helps us. You and I may live and breathe this message of redemption; we might say, "Yeah, sure, of course God helps us. That is grace." But for our people, they have no one to hear that from but us. We have to *name* that message. We have to more robustly name God's grace. Only naming it opens the door to relationship with God.

The homily is not just an after-dinner talk to entertain. The homily is not a moment to remonstrate with people to be better. We are called to go deeper into relationship with the Lord. The purpose of preaching is to help our people encounter the living God. Filled with that Presence, as the baptized, we are all called to holiness. But we cannot arrive at holiness by ourselves. We need the strength of the Spirit. We *need* the power of God. *God is here with us*: the Ruler of the Universe is an active Presence in our lives. Please say so, over and over again! Those who are bombarded by secular messages of "redeemers" plead, "Help us to *see and taste and touch* the working of God!" Moralizing *about* holiness and discipleship is not the same as inviting our folks to *meet* the Teacher himself.[6]

Our Work as Preachers

We preachers *know* we are not the One who transforms people. Yet there is an important human role for us to play in what God wants to do. The Second Vatican Council taught us that the presence of Christ in the liturgy is fourfold: Christ is visibly present

- in the gathered assembly,
- in the Word,
- in the Church's minister, and
- in the eucharistic species (*Sacrosanctum Concilium* 7).

The third and fourth elements, the presence of Christ in the Church's minister and in the bread and wine become Body and Blood of Christ, have often been highlighted in teaching about the Eucharist. Yet in recent years, there also has been discussion of the sacramental character of the Word: the Word effects what it signifies, mediating the encounter with God.[7] So what about the presence of Christ in the homilist, the preacher of the Word? What does that mean for our identity as *preacher*?

In the sacramentality of the preaching, your words are iconic, a window through which the face of God is revealed. As the Spirit bubbles within you, your face lights up with joy. Your hands exude energy. Audible words proclaim an inaudible reality just as surely as the concrete eucharistic elements lead the people to "see" the unfathomable depths of God. Symbolically, when you stand to preach, with two hands open in front of you, you hold the community in your hands and then reverently, slowly, and homiletically lift that *us* (by naming the experiences, hopes, struggles, fears) to God.[8]

This homiletic image is much like the elevation of the elements at the great Amen of the Eucharistic Prayer, yet it is your people's lives, not the bread and wine, that you raise. Then, moving from God to the people, you offer the divine realities as concrete words to your people. Lead the discouraged from despair to hope. Help your people to meet that Someone who brings them from floundering to dwelling secure, from condemnation to being embraced, and from feeling distanced to drawing close.

The purpose of our preaching is this encounter with the God who saves us all. As a result of this graced back-and-forth dance, the Holy Spirit as Connector draws together preacher and people, and then through the preaching lifts all to God. Through this interaction, then, the homily itself is a movement of prayer, an integral element of the prayer of the Mass.

The dying and rising of Christ parallels everyday life. In Jesus's story, we recognize our own story. It is a narrative written into our lives, and into the earth itself. The same Holy Spirit power who propelled Jesus through everyday life in Nazareth to the Cross and Resurrection is here for us. Everyday life is full of dark and death-dealing moments. Life is rich with resurrection experiences. So in Paschal Mystery preaching, we name three things: (1) we name the darkness, (2) we name the light, and (3) we explicitly identify the movement of the One who transforms the darkness to light and death to life. We bring the three elements together—the joys, the struggles, and the workings of God. There are enough everyday variations of the Paschal Mystery that a preacher should never need to ask, "So . . . what can I preach today?"[9] Rather the preacher attunes eyes, ears, heart, and mind to the Paschal Mystery all around.

We are called to preach in such a way that hearts are set "on fire with praise and thanksgiving" for what the Redeemer of redeemers has done (and is doing) for us.[10]

We want the Holy Spirit to work through us to bring our people to an encounter with God. We want to help them find their way to an encounter with divine love. "Encounter is God's very *method* of salvation."[11] We want them to *know* the God who made, saves, and sustains them. Effective liturgical preaching for encounter says to our hearers, "Here is the door. Walk through it into the arms of the One who is Mercy."

Discuss and Reflect

1. As you think about preaching the Paschal Mystery, where else do the people to whom you preach (especially those on the margins) turn for a "redeemer"? Sports? Coffee? Work? Mountain climbing? Alcohol? Netflix? What else aims to fill the God-sized hole in each person?

2. How are you and your words iconic, a window into God? How do you feel about being a window into God? Where is the "window" dirty? How do you find fresh ideas to be an icon?

3. Look ahead to the "Try This" section and the "Read or View" suggestions below. Which of those do you discern as something you would like to try, read, or view to help you grow as a window into God?

Try This!

Create a Paschal Mystery Homily

When we preach the Paschal Mystery, we name

- the darkness—the ways our people (including ourselves) are experiencing death in both everyday and extraordinary events and circumstances;

- the light—the ways resurrection is experienced by our people in everyday life; and

- the encounters our people have with God, the agent of transformation, the One who makes that transformation happen.

If we fail to offer this explicit and rich language, we are implying that people have to lift themselves up by their own bootstraps, giving them no person to turn to, no one more powerful than themselves, no one to trust, no Redeemer! That deeply involved and caring Someone is what makes Christianity distinct from the secular world and its myriad of would-be redeemers.

In preaching, we must *always* name the grace, the One, the Holy, who brings us from the dark to the light and from death to life. Therefore, at the core of our proclamation, we preach the transformation made possible through the Paschal Mystery.

1. With the chart on the next page in hand, reflect on the scriptures you will preach on in this upcoming week, or weeks.

2. Where is there darkness in the passage? What are the struggles of the characters? How does the wrestling of the biblical community relate to the struggles of those who will gather in your pews to listen to your preaching? If the passage contains only light, what is its opposite? What might make your people push back or resist the message of the text?

3. As you read the passage, what is the opposite of its darkness? Where is the Good News, the light, the antidote to the darkness? What is the itch you'd like your preaching to scratch? How can you express this Good News in ordinary, everyday concrete language? (Notice that it is easier to describe bad news than it is to talk concretely about Good News. The psalms are often a good source for descriptive language for the working of God. Avoid familiar or overused platitudes.)

4. How is God at work in this scripture? What is God doing and how? Name explicitly which person of the Trinity is at work if you can. How does the activity of God in the text relate to what is happening in the lives of your people?

Choose one row in the chart (or add one of your own) on which to center your homily—one element of darkness, light, and agency.

To Preach the Paschal Mystery in the World of Human Experience

From an experience of death/darkness	Through the agency of God	To an experience of life/light
1. Heartache		1. Splendor
2. Abandoned		2. Supported
3. Judged		3. Accepted
4. Sorrow		4. Joy
5. Weary		5. Refreshed
6. Shock		6. Reassure
7. Distance		7. Draw close
8. Muddy		8. Clear
9. Uncertain		9. Sure
10. Dismiss		10. Embrace
11. Despairing		11. Hope
12. Frustrated	God the Father, Son, and Holy Spirit causes the transformation to happen.	12. Fulfilled
13. Suffering	• How?	13. Peace
14. Controlled	• Where?	14. Surrendered
15. Waffling	• Why?	15. Standing
16. Condemned	• With whom?	16. Embraced
17. Rejected	• What does that look like?	17. Chosen
18. Desolate		18. Fruitful
19. Evade		19. Face
20. Drowning		20. Rescued
21. Torn down		21. Built up
22. Bore		22. Touch
23. Deny		23. Admit
24. Thirst		24. Overflow
25. Silenced		25. Heard
26. Flounder		26. Dwell secure
27. Quit		27. Persevere
28. Trick		28. Clarify
29. Perplex		29. Solve
30. Separate		30. Join
(Add yours here)		(Add yours here)
Tie in . . . Name the human struggle	Name the agent of transformation	. . . and stretch Bring us to the Good News

Read or View

Read or view additional materials found in this companion folder: https://bit.ly/RememberingWhyWePreach or use this code:

The materials for this chapter include the following:

Peter John Cameron, "The Method: Preaching Is an Encounter," chap. 2 in *Why Preach? Encountering Christ in God's Word*, 47–66 (San Francisco: Ignatius Press, 2009).

Sample homilies: St. Augustine's Easter Sermon 229A and Fr. Mike Connors's Easter Vigil homily. All materials used with permission.

Suggested Reading for Further Study

If you'd like to dig deeper into preaching the Paschal Mystery and preaching as worship, try the following:

Connors, Michael E. "Preaching as Worship: Progress and Ongoing Issues in Roman Catholicism." *Church Life* 2, no. 3 (January 2014). https://churchlifejournal. nd.edu.

Connors, Michael E., and Ann M. Garrido. "Doctrinal and Catechetical Preaching." In *A Handbook for Catholic Preaching*, edited by Edward Foley, 124–33. Collegeville, MN: Liturgical Press, 2016.

DeLeers, Stephen Vincent. "The Homily as Liturgical Word: The Assembly and Its Sacred Ritual." Chapter 5 in *Written Text Becomes Living Word*, 69–85. Collegeville, MN: Liturgical Press, 2004.

Driscoll, Jeremy. "Preaching the Resurrection: Central Content of the New Evangelization." In *To All the World: Preaching and the New Evangelization*, edited by Michael E. Connors, 139–53. Collegeville, MN: Liturgical Press, 2016 (or watch Fr. Driscoll's address of the same title at https://youtu.be/YgQ6AMecv90).

Waznak, Robert. *An Introduction to the Homily*, 20–23. Collegeville, MN: Liturgical Press, 1998.

3.

Preaching as a Spiritual Practice

As we seek to lead our people deeper into an encounter with the living God, we ourselves seek to pray even more deeply than we preach. We go to the desert on our peoples' behalf to discern, "Lord, what do your people need to hear now? What do you want me to tell them?" Preaching that inspires is brought into existence through preparation filled with listening, prayer, and study.

The Preacher as Witness

> I don't know Who—or what—put the question, I don't know when it was put. I don't even remember answering. But at some point, I did answer "yes" to Someone—or Something—and from that hour I was certain that existence is meaningful and that, therefore, my life, in self-surrender, had a goal.
>
> —Dag Hammarskjöld, secretary-general of the United Nations
> (1953–1961)[1]

As Hammarskjöld writes in his final journal entry, *Someone* moved in his life. That loving encounter gave him meaning. That encounter gave him purpose. He could have said no to the One who called him. But he found that his yes made a profound difference.

27

As with Hammarskjöld, God has changed *us*. Thus, our lives, in self-surrender, also have a goal: to be true to the One who calls us, to speak of who it is that gives us life. We become witnesses. Pope Paul VI said, "Modern man listens more willingly to witnesses than to teachers, and if he does listen to teachers, it is because they are witnesses" (*Evangelii Nuntiandi* 41).

The first move, then, in "preaching for encounter" is to turn inward to deepen our own spiritual lives. If we seek to lead our people toward a deeper encounter with the living God, then we preachers must also spend time opening ourselves to deeper encounter with God. Pope Francis suggests in *Evangelii Gaudium*,

> Whoever wants to preach must be the first to let the Word of God move him deeply and become incarnate in his daily life. In this way preaching will consist in that activity, so intense and fruitful, which is "communicating to others what one has contemplated." (150)

We have met preachers who consistently bring people into an encounter with Jesus. They have one thing in common: they radiate with their eyes, their smile, and their words one message. In the pulpit and out, effective preachers exude this simple reality: I have met Jesus. He has changed my life. I want you to meet him too.

Thus, our goal is to pray even better than we preach.[2] When we have prayed in the spiritual depths, the vibrancy we experience will resonate through our preaching. As we encounter the divine, the joy of that meeting will shine through our delivery and our words. God is good. That holy interaction will bubble into the smile lines of our faces, the vigor of our bodies, and the passion in our voices. If we strive to inspire conversion through our preaching, we must first undergo our own conversion. We ourselves have to be willing to be touched and changed by God.

Preaching Preparation as a Spiritual Discipline

The most difficult homily to preach is the message that we pass on by the way we live our daily lives. Our parishioners see us in and out of the pulpit. They will find us credible in the pulpit on Sunday when they witness our holiness in the office, the school, the hospital, and on the streets on the other days. Prayer and preaching, life and liturgy, all have to line up. Pope Francis says, "The Sunday readings will resonate in all their brilliance in the hearts of the faithful if they have first done so in the heart of their pastor" (*Evangelii Gaudium* 149).

Yet a life of everyday holiness is not easy. In coaching preachers, we have heard of many challenges: the life of ministry is busy, moments for study disappear, extended silence for reflection is nonexistent, and time for prayer is limited. Many clergy lament that the first thing to disappear after seminary is the opportunity to pray and study.[3]

In addition, some priests and deacons have found that seminary training and ordination did not make them the homilists they had hoped to be. Some have survived by faking it. A few have gotten by on natural talent. Others rationalize that their preaching is good enough (or at least better than most). Some preachers admit that months can go by without them saying a word that could convert even them, preaching the same stale platitudes over and over again. Some have said they can be "dead preachers walking, but the most devastating thing is that nobody seems to notice. Nobody seems to care or hold [us] accountable."[4]

Part of the renewal process you have opted into with this book is support. How can you work toward holiness of life? Whether you are working alone or in a group, have someone to check in with monthly who will ask, "Where are you with God today?" and "How can you deepen your spiritual life as a preacher so your words arise from a heart deeply in tune with the Holy Spirit?" and "How do *you* encounter God?" These support companions will keep you accountable. Someone has to check in to make sure you are not a dead preacher walking. Your spiritual health matters. Spiritual renewal is the foundation of preaching for encounter.

"Deep calls to deep" (Ps 42:7). From our own depths, we speak of the living, mysterious, and personal Divine Presence whom we have met, so we can invite our hearers into that same deep experience. We want to lead them to know the intimate God who dwells with us.

So how do we do this? Faithful preparation for preaching becomes a distinct spiritual discipline. It calls for a rhythm of prayer, discernment, study, composition, editing, and practice. This unique homiletic spirituality can be both learned and grown.

Moments set aside for study and prayer may become *the* primary locus for spiritual growth. To create that space has to be intentional, deliberate. Make it a priority. God wants to meet your people, through you. Someone's life may depend on it. Our prayer cannot be about *only* the next homily—sometimes we need to pray just to spend time with our Beloved—but we dare not preach without prayer.

A Pastor's Prayer

So what does a preacher's prayer look like? In seminary, many students learn prayer forms that originated in monastic life—the Liturgy of the Hours, daily Mass, and structured times for reflection and adoration. Once tossed into demanding parish life, those prayer elements still remain important. But busy pastors cannot be monks. The busier we are, the more we need to pray. Those who minister learn to pray with, in, and through the activities of daily work and ministry. Experienced preachers learn to pray and listen to God on the drive to the hospital to anoint a dying friend. Prayer may mean setting aside three minutes to walk down the street and praise God for the beauty of the clouds. Prayer may mean saying a Rosary as one falls asleep. The life of parish ministry is active. Thus we learn to become what St. Ignatius of Loyola called "contemplatives in action."[5]

The discernment of preaching also has a special kind of creativity and attentiveness: we "pray as we go." The Holy Spirit speaks in all times and places, sometimes surprisingly: The scriptures simmer within us as we brush our teeth. Reading the news sparks an "aha!" that offers the key to Sunday's message. A stray comment at a high school football game gives us an insight into how fifteen-year-olds think. The Word became flesh and was immersed fully in human life. To connect with our people, we also have to know how and where they live; we have to "get a life."[6] We learn to develop an observant eye for the way God moves in ordinary ways and an ear inclined to the voices of God's people. This incarnational perspective invites attentiveness to the working of God in ordinary events. We seek to become mystics of everyday life.[7] This becomes the homiletic lens through which we see the world.

For that homiletic lens to be focused, we have to read the next Sunday's scripture early in the week so that the Word walks with us as we walk among our people. Three or four homilies may be simmering in our upcoming-preaching crockpots—thoughts for funerals and weddings and school Masses run around in our brains. This can be a mentally taxing. Yet at the same time, the gospel invigorates life! All of these flashes and ponderings can be prayer: we lift our minds to the Lord as the inspirations arise.

The Temptation to "Mine for a Message"

One of the preaching temptations we have seen too often is impatience with the Holy Spirit: a preacher wants to mine a message out of the scripture readings. An indicator of this temptation is when the first question a homilist asks of the scriptural text is, "What am I going to say?" The mental allure sounds like this: "I already know what this reading says" and/or "It is obvious what I have to preach, and I can pull that message out in a few minutes." That enticement can grow as a preacher gains in years: the scriptures become hyper-familiar, even almost overlearned. Thus, the underlying attitude about preaching can grow to become "I know this" and "I've got this." For example, for the

Feast of the Baptism of the Lord, a preacher might immediately conclude, "Well, this is about baptism. I'll preach about baptism."

But what does the Lord want to say to this people in this moment through you, his preacher? Is that superficiality going to be faithful to the Lectionary readings? When you find yourself starting to mine, stop! Wait. Take your time. Don't fall for the temptation of "What am *I* going to say to them?" (Notice that the subject of that sentence is *I*.) Homiletic discernment means to prayerfully listen, to offer your voice and your words to the God who wants to speak. The point of preaching is to be in service to this: What does *God* want to say?

Gathering Ideas with Scripture and Prayer

Homiletic discernment works like this: start early, listen, take a few days to pray and study, let ideas arise with you, and slowly craft ideas. Let the Holy Spirit transform *you* as you read the passages. Otherwise, your preaching will grow stale: you will get bored and your preaching will be boring. Let the Word, who is living and active, move within *you* first. Take the time to pray and listen.

One method of praying with scripture is lectio divina. Here are a few of the many types:

- *Personal lectio divina.* As you prayerfully read the scripture passages, ask this: What moves you personally? What words or phrases from the lection stand out for you? What would you like to learn more about? Where is the Lord spiritually challenging you to grow deeper through the passage?

- *Congregational lectio divina.* As you read, imagine that you are a particular member of your congregation. How does that person hear the pericope? What personal struggles might these words address? What words of hope does the Lord have?

- *Action/verb lectio divina.* Read the passage with particular attention to the verbs. Circle or underline the verbs. Look at their tense—present, past, or future? What is the action in this passage? What is the Lord doing? How is God actively at work? What are the various people doing?

- *Ignatian contemplation.* Place yourself in the scene. What does it feel like to be one of the characters? An inanimate object? A particular animal or plant? What do the surroundings feel like, taste like, and sound like? Be playful in your imagination. Let the Holy Spirit open the eyes of your mind and your senses as you walk around the scene.

Prayer and Preaching Come Together for the Faith of Our People

You cannot think and play with and ponder the scriptures forever. At some point, you have to get the homily done. All of those simmering pieces have to come together at a time of formal preparation. We trust the Holy Spirit to guide us in this focused part of the process as well. Pope Francis entreats us to prepare carefully:

> Preparation for preaching is so important a task that a prolonged time of study, prayer, reflection and pastoral creativity should be devoted devoted to it. . . . [There is a] need to devote quality time to this precious ministry. Some pastors argue that such preparation is not possible given the vast number of tasks which they must perform; nonetheless, I presume to ask that each week a sufficient portion of personal and community time be dedicated to this task, even if less time has to be given to other important activities. Trust in the Holy Spirit whose work during the homily is not merely passive but active and creative. It demands that we offer ourselves and all our abilities as instruments (cf. Rom 12:1) which God can use. A preacher who does not prepare is not "spiritual"; he is dishonest and irresponsible with the gifts he has received. (*Evangelii Gaudium* 145)

The "preciousness of the ministry of preaching" obliges us to take the time needed for careful preparation. You may find that you have too many ideas at this point and you'll need to edit rigorously.[8] You may find that you have too few ideas and you need to expand upon them to create a homily. So, first look at the content of what you are going to say.

Recall that our goal is to evoke an encounter with the living God. Therefore, the words we use to preach should have spiritual depth. What kinds of words, images, and content evoke this encounter with God? Consider those who will hear you. What words, what sort of language, will help them meet God? The great spiritual writers and preachers crafted images and used words that led their followers to God. Does that mean you as a preacher have to become a poet, a mystic, and a great saint?

Hopefully, yes, we are all headed that way. But even while we are still limping along on that journey, we can broaden our spiritual vocabulary. We can bolster our modes of expression so we strengthen our ability to communicate the Gospel. The people of God are not needing a seven-course poetic feast from our words. But a peanut butter sandwich that nourishes faith would be most welcome.

Turn with us for a moment to get a taste of the language of spirituality; this will inform what and how we are to speak on God's behalf.

The Language of Spirituality

Christian preaching is *always paschal* in content. The suffering and death of life are real. Our people come wounded. They come with questions: How can the God of love be present in the brokenness of life? Where is God found? How can this happen? We too have experienced failures and weakness. In humility before our God, we recognize that we also need a savior, a redeemer, someone to lift us up. We come together as one with them. The language of spirituality is the language of *we*. God can use our failures to bring us closer to him. We voice our people's concerns. We offer a word of pardon and healing. In solidarity, we all hunger to extract meaning from our experience. Our role as a preacher is to be a mediator of meaning for our people.[9] This mediation will be a permanent feature of our preaching. Paschal preaching takes seriously the *experiences of sin, doubt, and struggle.*

As we mentioned in the last chapter, paschal preaching always points to the One who brings us from death to life. We do not have to live this difficult life on our own. We do not walk the Christian walk all by ourselves.

As we preachers grow more filled with the goodness and grandeur of God, our preaching will become transformational, overflowing with joy and hope. The Resurrection of Christ means victory over sin and death! The Resurrection is the cornerstone of the spiritual life of which we speak. Easter assures us of God's power even in the mundane things of life. We reveal the living, risen Christ who walks among us. We always point to God, to hope, to eternal life, and to never-ending joy. We experience resurrection in large and small ways. In our preaching, we name that hope and describe daily experiences of resurrection. The spiritual language for our preaching is paschal. We are preachers with hope to bring.

We speak of hope and resurrection, joy and eternity. Yet these abstractions have to be translated into everyday language—*incarnational* language holds together body and spirit, this world and the next. Ordinary words can affirm the graciousness of bodiliness and the material world—it all comes from God.

Appeal to and integrate the whole of human experience into your homilies: mind, heart, will, senses, imagination, and community. As people of the earth, we experience God through the sacramental imagination; the visible, created world leads us to the invisible Creator. God's gracious presence is mediated through all things living. This includes the Church and its rites (especially the Eucharist). It also includes God's

Presence through the Word, through other people, through the human community, through artistic expression and story, and through the natural world—through all of human experience. We communicate so that our people grow new eyes and a more penetrating vision.

We use concrete words. We interweave ordinary metaphors and images from family and work. We use stories of daily living as Jesus did. In short, we use the *experiential* language of spirituality. We have a living, mysterious, and Divine Presence here with us. We use simple and accessible, everyday language. We talk about the reality that we can communicate with God and God wants to communicate with us. We invite our people into the depths of our own rootedness with God.

The language of spirituality also speaks from the Christian mystical tradition. Spiritual writers are good resources for preaching. Our words can respect and nurture both the *kataphatic* and the *apophatic* dimensions of spiritual life, to create a balance between word and wordlessness. Preaching can show the way to the deep and prayerful quiet of apophatic contemplation. Profound silence is appropriate within the liturgy, of which the homily is integral. There can be pauses when the words of preaching cease; we allow the Holy Spirit to invite us into a silence that God alone can fill. Our words do not have to do all the work. The experience of the divine starts with God's initiative. We can evoke, clarify, intensify, and communicate that experience, but we cannot create it. God alone is enough.

Going to the Desert on Their Behalf

Ideally, when we rise to speak to our gathered communities, we have prayed, we have wrestled with the scriptural texts, and we have begged a word from the Lord for them. We have gone to the desert on their behalf. This prayerful preparation is an act of love for them and for the One who sends us to draw them into encounter.

In the moment of preaching itself, when at our best, we exude the joy of our own encounter with God in these scriptures. We preach as if to say, "I want to be here with you. I have wrestled with this too, and it means a lot to me; what I am offering to you is my gift to you." The prayerful quality of such preaching is not lost on our listeners; such homiletic authenticity is irreplaceable in its ability to invite our hearers into an encounter with the living God.

In summary, to be a preacher is not just to be the communicator of a message at Mass. Preaching is not a task or responsibility to put on and take off like an alb or a stole. To be a preacher is a way of life. We are to be prayer-filled witnesses of God's presence and constant offer of intimate relationship. To be a witness or conduit for others implies a profound humility; we too are on the way. We bear witness to the journey that we ourselves are willing to take. Thus, we as preachers are called to be spiritual leaders to guide others toward God. And there are few joys in our ministry as profound as when we know that God is at work as a hearer says to us, "Your homily touched my life."

Discuss and Reflect

1. Praying your way through the preparation of a homily—is that a customary practice for you? If so, how does that bear fruit in your preaching? If not, how could it become so? As you try the various forms of lectio divina, note how and why those inspire you.

2. How would you describe a "homiletic lens" on life? How is it a way of "seeing" differently? How do you experience the homily "simmering" within you as you go about your everyday life? And how does, or could, the language of spirituality enter into your preaching?

3. Look ahead to the "Try This" section and the "Read or View" suggestions in the next few pages. Which of those do you discern as something that would stretch you and help you to grow?

Try This!

A prayerful preparation process integrates preaching with study, spirituality, observing everyday life, discernment, writing, and editing. Give yourself time to carefully work through each of these as you prepare your next homily. Then ponder, With which of these elements do I most struggle? (An old coaching adage tells us, "Train your weaknesses and race your strengths.") Use all six in your preparation process, but pick one of these (your weakest) to focus on this next month.

Contemplation

I prayerfully engage with the text (by myself or with a group).

- *Pray.* I read the text, I pray, and I listen to the Holy Spirit. What is the Spirit saying? What stands out for me?

- *Contemplate.* I allow the scripture passages to prayerfully simmer within me as I go about my daily life.

- *Discuss.* I share the fruits of my contemplation with others and listen for how they hear the passage.

Observation

- What am I seeing and hearing? What am I perceiving differently in everyday life as these scriptures simmer in my homiletic crockpot of ideas?

- Increase your knack for noticing: What thought floaters go through your mind as you walk around each day?

- What is the Lord saying to you or showing you in relation to this homily?

- Look carefully at something you take for granted. How can you see this with the fresh eyes of this week's homiletic lens?

Study

What intrigues, unsettles, or arouses curiosity in me about this scripture passage? What do I want to investigate further? Go and find what others have learned.

- *Scripture study.* Use biblical methods to dig more deeply into the direction and questions raised through prayer: What do the scholars/others have to say about it? What can I learn that I didn't know before? Investigate a word, a Bible character, a geography, a context, a historical situation, poetry, music, and so forth—whatever strikes your curiosity. (Keep learning! Weekly snippets of education over a lifetime lead to a learned and wise preacher.)

- *Theological study.* What does this mean to me? What are my theological presuppositions as the preacher? In the context in which I will be preaching this, what are the theological presuppositions of those who will hear this scripture? What can I incorporate from the tradition of the Church?

Write and Prepare to Preach

- How do I craft and then proclaim a focused gospel message that has a carefully constructed form that leads my people toward God?

- What do I discern as God's purpose for this particular homily or reflection?

- What's the one pearl of great price that I will serve up? (Focus)

- What does the Holy Spirit want the homily to accomplish through me and my words? What do I want my words to *do* in the hearer? (Function)

- Write out a rough draft (even if you do not ordinarily use a manuscript for preaching). Then think about the way in which you have arranged the images, declarative statements, discursive elements, and other pieces together.

- Think through this: What do I need to move around? How do I construct this particular message so that it best accomplishes its purpose? Try switching parts around, asking, how am I best going to get my people toward the function of this homily? (Form)

    Note: We will give more input on focus, function, and form in chapter 5.

Edit and Practice

We have found that many Sunday preachers preach a rough draft, or not even a rough draft. Many homilies are a collection of loose ideas somehow strung together. Editing is *vital* to effective preaching!

- Listener complaints include "please, make one point," "speak clearly," and "relate to me," and can be attributed to the lack of making time for editing. Many preachers struggle to find the time in their busy schedules to edit carefully. Yet it is the refining process that shapes and reshapes the message for effective preaching.

- Practice the homily aloud. Where does "the flow" get stuck? Edit there.

- Preachers who have been at their craft for a long time can get in a rut. They are strong in some ways, weak in others. They often use the same form and/or the same words and phrases over and over again. Use the feedback form in appendix 2 as a personal checklist for the editing of your homily:

- Look especially for

    » unity/coherence,
    » a structure that can be followed, and
    » a central point that clearly speaks to the listeners and relates to their lives.

- In which areas on the form do I consistently do well?

- What elements are consistently missing from my homilies?

- Where do I need to grow?

    » Pick one move or paragraph to strengthen according to the ideal characteristics described in the evaluation form. If you have time, strengthen a second section as well.

Read or View

Read or view additional materials found in this companion folder: https://bit.ly/RememberingWhyWePreach or use this code:

The materials for this chapter include the following:

John Donne, "Holy Sonnet No. 14."

Bishop Robert Morneau's chapter "Preaching as a Spiritual Exercise," in *A Handbook for Catholic Preaching*, ed. Edward Foley, 3–13 (Collegeville, MN: Liturgical Press, 2016).

Sample homilies by Karla Bellinger and Pope Francis. All materials used with permission.

Suggested Reading for Further Study

Cressman, Lisa. *Backstory Preaching: Integrating Life, Spirituality and Craft*. Collegeville, MN: Liturgical Press, 2018.

Taylor, Barbara Brown. *The Preaching Life*. Lanham, MD: Rowman & Littlefield, 1993 (especially chapter 1).

Wallace, James A. "Cultivating the Preacher's Hunger: 'To Make the Lord Known and Loved,'" chap. 6 in *Preaching to the Hungers of the Heart: The Homily on Feasts and within the Rites*, 175–94. Collegeville, MN: Liturgical Press, 2002.

Westerhoff, John. *Spiritual Life: The Foundation for Preaching and Teaching*. Louisville, KY: Westminster Press, 1994.

4.

Preaching as a Pastoral Practice

We believe that the Lord is present in the community, the Body of Christ. He calls all the faithful, both ordained and lay together, to conversion and a flourishing of life. Thus, to preach is a pastoral practice of care for a particular community. Yet our communities are changing. People of today hear differently, as the whole world is in the middle of a communication shift. So how do we discern how to effectively preach to these people at this time in our own particular communities?

A Spirituality of Community

In the 1982 document *Fulfilled in Your Hearing*, the US bishops opened their document on preaching by writing about listeners. They pointed to "the great emphasis which communication theorists place on an accurate understanding of the audience if communication is to be effective."[1] Effective communication begins with a healthy understanding of what is going on in the community.

Preaching is a communal act. As we strive to connect the message of the Gospel with the people we serve, we go together. "By deepening our relationship with Christ and experiencing his love, we renew our faith as disciples in a community of believers, grow in confidence in the truth of the Gospel, and then share our faith in Jesus Christ joyfully with others."[2] Preaching and evangelization thus go together. We preach on Sunday so our people will go out and preach on Monday . . . and beyond.[3] As preachers who are discerning what the Lord wants us to say to one specific community at one specific moment, we need to know about how people are listening in our contemporary culture.

How Listeners Listen Today

Like other forms of public speaking, the homily has become a rare form of communication. Lecturing has fallen out of favor in higher education. Rhetoric, which was once considered the highest form of communication, has almost disappeared from the world of performance. You, as a preacher, send (what may feel like) a monologue from the pulpit each Sunday morning. This experience is not familiar to today's listener. Some may easily absorb your words. Some may not.

   People are listening to oral messages differently. That cultural communication shift influences us as preachers. What is going on?

- *People tune out.* There is so much noise. Messages bombard us. As a result, we tighten the intake valve and only take in what pertains to us. You probably experience this yourself: of all the information that comes at you on a daily basis, how much can you actually hear or read and listen to? We learn to select what matters to us and tune out the rest.

- *Listeners talk back.* Though the homily appears to be a monologue, effective preachers sense that communication is a two-way conversation. Listeners process your message: they nod *yes.* Yet they push back and resist. Even at times they internally say *no* to what you are saying. You may think your homily is brilliant, but if their verdict is that it is over their heads or boring, they simply will not hear you. For better and for worse, our current culture expects two-way interaction. To give you an example, the second time that my (Karla's) twelve-year-old granddaughter went to Mass, the homilist asked what was supposed to be a rhetorical question. Sophie answered him aloud—actually rather loudly—to her grandmother's embarrassment. She *expected* interaction. She was not used to listening silently. Someone asked a question, and Sophie responded. Many of us internally respond to messages, both *yes* and *no* and sometimes *maybe.* Albeit usually more quietly. Or we talk back inside, silently.

- *We see.* We are becoming a visual world, rich in pictures that come at us in a flash—on cell phones and computers, in movies and on television.[4] This is as true in India as it is in Canada. Our mental pathways adapt to that quick visual pace. As a result, we may process oral speech more poorly. When a group of people talk about what sticks in their minds, memories are mostly image laden. We don't hear well. We visualize; we see.

- *We feel.* In our culture, we have grown used to being persuaded by impressions; many of us pick a candidate by how he or she makes us feel rather than by the logic of his or her argument. We are not accustomed to processing the finer points of a spoken argument, proposed plan, or complex solutions presented in didactic or expository language. Rather, we are most easily influenced by the persuader's selection of stories, the emotive tug of the words chosen, and the mood established by environment and presentation. Marketers have researched how to manipulate our feelings to get us to buy a product or commit to a cause. Communications have become more subjective. We don't so often analyze a train of thought. We sense; we feel.

Tune out, talk back, see, and feel—does this cultural shift mean that preaching is passé or obsolete as a way to transmit the Gospel? Is the homily outdated, archaic, and out of date as a mode of communication? No! Thus far, the Holy Spirit has not allowed preaching to fade away. In every age of history, as culture has changed, preaching has adapted, but the Word of God has not been silenced.[5]

Historically, in the early years of a communication shift, there were moments when the way of passing on the Gospel had not yet caught up to cultural changes. At those junctures, there was real concern that the faith would fade away. Right now, there is plenty of worry that faith will fade away. So, how can the words of a preacher carry weight in this new environment?

Surprisingly, in my (Karla's) study of young peoples' connection with Sunday preaching,[7] not one high school youth asked for more Facebook or Twitter from the grown-ups in their lives. They hungered, rather, for authentic, loving adults to take a focused interest in them. They hoped for preachers who would speak to them about how to make sense of their crazy world in the light of the Gospel of Jesus Christ. Some college administrators are finding the same: today's youth do not want to give up interpersonal interaction.[6] We have seen that online is not enough. Live interaction is needed. Teenagers' body language and verbal responses can send the contradictory messages of both "come close" and "go away." Yet with so much noise surrounding them, life is confusing. This yearning for personal interaction actually opens tremendous opportunities for a caring preacher. A preacher who is willing to believe in his people, cut through the noise, speak in visual images, and connect with the truth of the Gospel to bring his people closer to the living God has tremendous potential to make an impact.

We are preaching for transformation—theirs and our own (*Evangelii Gaudium* 9–10). To be transformed, listeners have to be receptive, properly disposed for the Word of God to sink in. How does that willingness come to be?

Motivation to Listen

You have some listeners who are prepared to hear you even *before* you begin to preach. Here's why they are approachable:

- They are deeply in love with God and hungry to hear what you can offer them. Their hearts may have already been warmed by prayer and/or the reading of the scriptures.

- They have had kindhearted experiences of your faith community.

- They have formed a positive impression of you or a personal relationship with you as a preacher outside of the setting of Mass; this could be in the context of confession or pastoral counseling or hospital visits. It could be a friendly conversation in the back of the church or over coffee and donuts. When they have a prior connection with you, they listen differently. You have already spoken to their hearts. They are ready to hear more from you.

- They are at some kind of a turning point in their lives. They have some need, some pain, a question, some breakdown, or an inadequacy in their heart or mind. In moments of trial and transition and doubt, folks grapple with, "Where is God in this moment?" The embers of faith inside of them are ready to be stirred into flame by your preaching.

Other listeners will listen to you more carefully *as* you speak. Here's why they begin to listen:

- They perceive that "this message pertains to me and my life." You take them on a pathway of discovery to questions that matter to them.

- They see that you are authentic and interesting. They are drawn in by the way you craft your words and the conversational way you deliver them.

- They sense you are also involved in the struggle of life. Since you are preaching to yourself as much as to them, they see that this message is personal; this "God stuff" matters to you.

- The homily offers them the possibility of a real encounter with God the Father, with Jesus the Christ, or with the Holy Spirit. You show them that this could be a real relationship to enter into and/or you show them the way forward toward deepening that relationship.

- For those who are at a turning point in their lives, they sense that your words address their need, offer them hope or a way forward, or give them a different perspective on their difficulties.

These are overall factors of listener receptivity that lead to an encounter with God. As you are preparing your homily, what can you consciously do to create pathways through which transformation comes?

Pathways to Listening

Conversion arises from the Holy Spirit. We experience inspired "aha!" moments. They can come through nature, in adoration, through liturgy, or via music. But the homily can also be a conduit for inspiration. What does that look like?

No two people are the same. A father and son can be sitting next to each other in a pew; one thinks the homily is inspiring, and the other is totally bored. Why is that? People are moved in different ways. "Ahas" come from streams of connection that flow together to run into the larger river of conversion. What are those streams of connection?

Each person is an integration of mind (analysis and imagination), heart, and will. When we craft a message that fires on all of these pathways, we tie in to the theologically holistic way that God has created us to be. Pope Francis alludes to this when he says, "A good homily, an old teacher once told me, should have 'an idea [the left brain], a sentiment [the heart], [and] an image [the right brain]'" (*Evangelii Gaudium* 157). St. Augustine would have added to that teacher's advice persuasion of the will, or moving the will to action.

We seek to make one point in our homily. But if all we have is a focus statement, how do we expand on that *one* point so we don't have to make *another* point to fill our time? Let us unpack these pathways so we can make our point to different people in different ways.

Left-Brain Thinkers

Logical (left-brain) thinkers are invigorated by a thoughtful and consistent line of reasoning. Check the rough draft of a homily you are working on. Even if you yourself are a heart-centered preacher and love to share a story, include depth of thought within that narrative. Is there one major theological point? Do your moves progress in a coherent and structured way? Will your hearers be stretched via a thought or an idea that energizes their thinking?

Right-Brained Imaginers

As we described earlier, in our increasingly visual society, many people are image based (right brain) as they receive communications: Do you have a central image that flows throughout your writing? Will your people see something they can remember? Does that visual weave into your main stream of thought, and then twist and turn throughout the homily? For example, if you are preaching about the call of the disciples along the seashore, water could become your unifying metaphor: whether showing up in images of the sea, the waters of baptism, the rain on the parish roof, or the drip of the bathroom sink, the image of water can tie your thoughts together.

In addition, as you have done your lectio divina prayer, have you pondered that central image and what it evokes in your own spiritual life, the life of the congregation, or in the gift of God? Is that metaphor one that you deeply envision, one that has been an inspiration and source of growth for you in your spiritual preparation for this homily? If that image has touched your life, you will be excited to preach it, and it will resound with your people when you speak it aloud.

Heart-Focused People

"I'm looking for something that touches me," a grandmother says. "I don't get anything out of it," a teenager complains. These two are seeking for a message that speaks to the heart. Check to see that somewhere in your homily, you speak to something that your people value deeply—a hunger, an ache, or an emotional need they have. Have you addressed that longing from our scriptures and our theology? Are you giving them some Good News to help them to flourish? To speak to the heart is not just to name the need but also to discover the benefit, the goodness, and the joy of the Gospel, which meets that need. In the transformation of the Paschal Mystery (review the "Try This" in chapter 2), is there an acknowledgment of the One who loves us and brings about that change? Even if you yourself are primarily a left-brain and analytic thinker, stretch yourself to make your homily speak to the deepest places of your own heart and theirs.

Move the Will

In *Evangelii Gaudium*, Pope Francis ties image and will together: "An attractive image makes the message seem familiar, close to home, practical and related to everyday life. A successful image can make people savor the message, awaken a desire and move the will towards the Gospel" (157).

"Move the will toward the Gospel!" How do we do that? Do you have parts in your homily that fire the will, call them to something more? To firm commitment? Do you have language that urges them to rise higher, or to meet a challenge with courage? Listeners want to *do something* with your message, no matter which pathway leads them to an encounter God. *Doing* is part of *knowing*. You want to provide suggestions to stimulate the will, but avoid being too dictatorial. Leave room for the Spirit to work.

Don't reduce moving the will to things that are too picayune, such as "let's all bring diapers to Mass next week." You can be that prescriptive in your closing remarks at Mass. Save the homily for creating an encounter with God. Same for the announcements; don't put them into the homily. This is God's holy space to speak to your people. Keep it so. In a homily on forgiveness, your hearers may not have been thinking about a superficial takeaway like bringing diapers. They may have been pondering something deeper and more life changing, such as talking to the brother to whom they have not spoken in ten years. Open the possibilities for action; at the same time, ask your people to reflect on how *they* can respond.

How does transformation ultimately happen? Lots of prayer: that "aha!" of conversion is the Holy Spirit's work to do. Your work is to set your homily on the mind, heart, and will pathways toward that encounter. Then pray for that encounter to happen—through you, a holy preacher of God. Effective preaching is an intensely local interaction. What matters to the people in your parish on this one particular Sunday? And how do you find out? In the next chapter, we will move toward opening that congregational conversation.

Discuss and Reflect

1. Think about those parishioners who are the inner core of your parish. They are the ones most likely to be most receptive to your preaching; they are also most likely to give you whatever feedback you get. Why do they listen as they do? Do they mention images that have stuck with them? Have you given them a thought on which they have commented? Have you touched their heart, given them hope or encouragement in some way?

2. Think about your own prayer life. Is there one pathway to God that you use most often? How could you integrate your own mind, heart, and will in prayer with more intentionality?

3. Look ahead to the "Try This" section and the "Read or View" after that. Which of those resonates with you as something you would like to try or do?

Try This!

Each preacher is a listener. Each preacher has certain pathways of listening that come most naturally to him or her. The way we ourselves process information affects how we structure our homilies. We may rely heavily on images that paint a mental picture, we may use discursive language to lay out a conscious line of reason and argument, or we may tell stories that speak to our own hearts. Yet what moves us as preachers may not be the same pathways that speak to our people. As we saw previously, an ideal homily has a good mix of mind, heart, and will.

In the coming month, be attentive to your own preferred mode of listening. When you watch a movie or read a book, analyze which of the pathways to connection you are most moved by: "I can see or imagine it!" (right brain); "I understand or get it!" (left brain); "I feel it or it touches me!"(heart); or "I want to do . . ." (will).

Now analyze one of your own homilies. Which pathway do you tend to use most often in your preaching? Identify where you are most comfortable and consistently lean. Look at how much of your homily speaks to the left brain, right brain, heart, and will.

For an upcoming homily, intentionally focus on creating a homily using one of the pathways in which you have traditionally been the *weakest*. If your homilies are customarily analytical, work on weaving in an image. If you are a storyteller who always appeals to the heart, add in a little doctrine for your left-brain people. If you typically leave people in their heads, speak to the will. Mix it up; train your weaknesses.

Experiment with the order of each of your elements. Some preachers begin with the head/analytical appeal, provide an image, build in a little heart appeal, and then tackle response/will. That is one way to structure a homily. But another sort of power can be released when we begin with heart or will/doing and then move to reflection or analysis. Create a mystery and walk along a path toward resolution. Weave all four elements into each of your moves within your structure.

Read or View

Read or view additional materials found in this companion folder: https://bit.ly/RememberingWhyWePreach or use this code:

The materials for this chapter include the following:

Karla J. Bellinger, "The World of the Listener," chap. 6 in *Connecting Pulpit and Pew: Breaking Open the Conversation about Catholic Preaching*, 78–91 (Collegeville, MN: Liturgical Press, 2014).

Michael E. Connors, "A Living Word of Hope for the Whatever Generation," afterword to *We Preach Christ Crucified*, 227–37 (Collegeville, MN: Liturgical Press, 2014). All materials used with permission.

Suggested Reading for Further Study

Atkinson, O'Brien. *How to Make Us Want Your Sermon: By a Listener*. New York: Joseph Wagner, 1942.

- The was the first book about preaching written from a listener point of view. Although about to disappear from print, this is a valuable, sometimes humorous, read.

Effective Preaching: What Catholics Want (DVD/CD). Leesburg, VA: National Catholic Educational Association, 2012.

- This study of listeners, complete with study guides, can be purchased at http://www.ncea.org.

Mulligan, Mary Alice, and Ronald J. Allen. *Make the Word Come Alive: Lessons from Laity*. St. Louis, MO: Chalice Press, 2005.

- This book is part of the four-volume series Channels of Listening, which arose from interviews with laypeople about what they are looking for in preaching.

Troeger, Thomas. *Imagining a Sermon*. Nashville: Abingdon, 1990.

- Troeger gives insight about how to become more visually and creatively imaginative.

PART II

Go Out!
A Life of
Leadership through
PREACHING

5.

Preaching as Spiritual Leadership

To be spiritual leaders, we must understand our people. When we know them, we will be able to lead them to the Good Shepherd. The preacher is a guide who discerns how and what to speak, when to support, and how to further growth and challenge.

The Preacher as Shepherd

At his first Chrism Mass, Pope Francis looked up from his prepared text. He said to the priests gathered, "This is what I am asking of you, be shepherds with the smell of sheep."[1] To be a spiritual leader means to be willing to spend the time to get smelly. We get to know our sheep and their needs. We carry them through dark valleys. We lead them forward to encounter the Good Shepherd. "To smell like our sheep" is a high calling.

What does being a shepherd mean for the way we preach? Spiritual leadership begins by knowing our community's relationship with God. Pope Francis writes, "The homily takes up once more the dialogue which the Lord has already established with his people. The preacher must know the heart of his community, in order to realize where its desire for God is alive and ardent, as well as where that dialogue, once loving, has been thwarted and is now barren" (*Evangelii Gaudium* 137). In the last section, we went inward to understand why we preach, our spiritual growth in preaching, Who it is we

57

preach, and to whom we preach. In this second half of the book, we look outward to who we are as we preach and how to connect and inspire the folks to whom we preach.

We have talked about the role of prayer in homily preparation. Our preaching as spiritual leaders builds from that prayer. As we listen for the moving of the Spirit, we also pay close attention to the community. We learn to recognize where and how the Lord is calling our people to grow. Spiritual leadership means to move someone through invitation, persuasion, and example, to move them from where they are to where God wants them to be. How do we do that?

The Discernment of Preaching

When we talked together after a workshop, a Byzantine pastor shared with me that he had just been transferred to a new parish and was struggling to connect with the people in his preaching. This wasn't his first experience of moving, however. He said, "When I move into a new parish, it takes me *five years* of careful listening to really understand how to preach to these particular people." This man did not assume that he knew how to preach to the people in his new parish—he had learned to be carefully attentive. Embracing the spirituality of preaching as a form of leadership means to grow deeply attuned to the needs of the other. This becomes a way of life.

What does it take to be deeply discerning? When you as a preacher live and breathe and eat with your people, you have the opportunity to learn their response styles, their dreams, their frustrations, and their hopes. Thus, you can discern how God is at work in their lives. You hold their lives sacred. Let us look at two elements of that discernment: (1) how to accompany our people on their paths and (2) how to discern where to guide and challenge them to grow closer to God.

A Spirituality of Accompaniment

Spiritual leadership begins by acknowledging that we are one with our people—we are not above them as the expert who knows all. We are with them on the journey of life: beset by similar limitations, filled with the same longings, and fired by comparable loves. When a listener responds after a homily, "You know my struggles and you fed my soul," you have connected.

That connection is the basis for a profound and essential act of trust that parishioners are willing to put in their preacher. Most people find it powerful to have their anxieties and concerns, desires and hopes, named. Doing this for your people signals that they and their lives are being taken seriously. This encourages them to believe that God is addressing them with a word of presence and power in that moment of your preaching. In the Spirit-initiated alliance between the preacher and his listeners, hope swells.

An integral part of prayerful preparation, then, is to look to see where and how the Spirit is at work:

- What words and phrases do my people use to describe their experiences of God?
- What stories of God's action do they tell?
- What life wisdom do they share with others?
- What are their confusions, longings, griefs, and sadnesses?
- What concrete experiences form their day-to-day lives?
- What do they value most?

Preaching the Mystery of Faith says, "Once he has come to know the customs, mores, practices, history, and religiosity of a people, a homilist can draw on that richness in order to make his presentation of the faith fresh and enlivening."[2]

The servant leadership of preaching asks us to lay aside our own agenda of "here's what *I* want to say" (a sender-side-focused message). We seek instead to discern what *God* wants to say to our people. Then we ask how that communication might be preached to be most deeply heard (a receiver-side-focused message). Knowing their language, symbols, and experiences, we can ask, how does *this* scriptural passage speak to *their* encounter with (or hunger for) God? What are they able to hear from us? Thus, the essential question for discernment in preaching is this: *What do these people need to hear from this text at this time and place through me, this preacher?*

As we accompany our people, we also recognize that we who are theologically educated have been immersed in a particular vocabulary. One of the first things a newly ordained priest has to learn is that the "churchy words" he used in seminary are not in common use. They have to be clarified. The core concepts of our faith—mercy, self-sacrifice, and goodness—have to be translated into what our people have experienced: not dumbed down, but made clear. If we don't do that, the response may be a shrug of "I don't get it." We cannot use abstract platitudes and be understood. We deliberately choose from *their* words for encounter, seeking for images and concepts *they* use in everyday life.

On the flip side of accompaniment is the other half of spiritual leadership: to discern what our people *do not* see or understand or live. To what *more* is God calling them? Our preaching is driven by, springs from, or taps into the experience of human longing and incompleteness. Yet it is not acceptable to simply leave people where they are.

To Guide and to Challenge

Ordination as priests and deacons deputizes us to lead God's people into the heart of the Father. As we get to know them, parishioners begin to trust us as someone who can show them where to go. They are looking for real value and rich meaning. When we stand at the ambo to read the Gospel and deliver a homily, both our person and our words are windows into God. The ministry of the Word is sacramental, including our preaching. Though sometimes we may want to, we cannot run away from that. We are an icon *through* whom our people look in order to encounter the divine. They are looking for how to find God amid the messy business of life. They don't expect us to have all the answers, but they *do* look to us as leaders who can help them keep their eyes on what is truly important. To be such a life guide is a high calling, almost scarily so. It makes preaching a momentous responsibility.

People in the pew *want* to know more of God.[3] From studies of listeners, they say, "Take us deeper, take us higher, and bring meaning to our lives." One of the biggest complaints about Catholic preaching, from both clergy and listeners, is that "preaching is too shallow." The spirituality of leadership takes seriously the depths of sin, doubt, and struggle. People grow impatient or bored with preaching that is superficial, lacks urgency, or remains abstract and remote from their lives. To strengthen them for life in this challenging world, we guide our people toward God.

Lead Us to the Mountain

You and I have experienced flashes of that encounter, haven't we? As holy witnesses, we can speak comfort from the God who met us in the warm wind by the ocean. We can witness to the God who roused us with courage when all seemed dark. We can speak about the One who offered unexpected new life through and beyond our death experiences. We can tell about the Spirit who grabbed us by the shirt collar to convict us of wrongdoing and pulled us onto a right path. We can open the imagination to the possibility of life lived differently, in God's presence. We can awaken visions of justice, compassion, hope, and love by witnessing to the divine *Someone* who cares about us. Someone who died for us. We can witness in our preaching to that Someone who is worth living and dying for!

When we put words to an experience of the heart, an "aha!" of the mind, or a conversion of the will, our people may remember their story of a similar experience and exclaim, "Oh! *That was God at work?*"[4]

We call our people to *more*. Good preachers believe in their people and their possibilities. Why? Because they know and believe the risen Lord is at work among them. Good preachers urge their listeners to follow and surrender and receive and drop everything and let go and trust and hope in the One who calls them—this spiritual challenge is the preacher's message. What does that spiritual leadership look like in the concrete practice of discerning what goes into a homily?

Discerning the Central Axis of the Homily

Unity of thought in the theme, structure, and flow of the homily is essential for understanding and lasting impact. Many homilies fail precisely here: they try to do too much, and don't hold together around a single point. Good preaching is focused, the memorable fruit of the preacher's prayerful openness to the Spirit.

Identify Homiletic Claims

As you pray and work with the scripture for your upcoming homily, begin to identify some possible main pathways that your homily could take. You may want to make yourself a list of possible *homiletic claims* that could form the main axis of the homily. Think of a homiletic claim as any reason your hearers might have for paying attention to this text or group of texts. A homiletic claim is *always* good news, and it always has God, one of the persons of the Blessed Trinity, as the *who*, the subject and actor.

Consider Preaching a Ministry of Discernment

You might even want to carry that list of possibilities around with you for a day or two, prayerfully considering which of those claims is what God wants to communicate at this moment. Preaching is, among other things, a ministry of discernment of the Holy Spirit's leading. We serve a living God who wants to speak to his people today as surely as he has spoken in the past. We are looking to preach a word that is not only true, good, and beautiful but also timely and contextual. This is what *Fulfilled in Your Hearing* describes as the preacher's role as "mediator of meaning."[5]

We are deputized to facilitate God's conversation with his people—this is no small thing! As homiletician Thomas Long says,

It is up to the preacher, then, to bring the life of the congregation into the text's presence, to dwell there long and prayerfully, and to discern the reality of this text as it is with us. [The result is neither abstract nor generic, but] more like personal address. It speaks to real people, and it wants a response.[6]

In a word, you are looking for the place where what the text says and does intersects with the needs and concerns of this community through your unique lens as preacher.

Discover the Needs of Your Community

Ask yourself, *What does this community at this time and place need to hear from this/ these text(s)?* As Long puts it, "The claim of the text is very occasion-specific; it is what we hear on *this* day, from *this* text, for *these* people, in *these* circumstances, at *this* juncture in their lives. Is there a word from the Lord *today*?"[7] We submit this to the guidance of the Holy Spirit, and when we've found it, it floods us with a peaceful and bold sense of, "Yes, this is what I must preach this Sunday."

Standing at the intersection of possibilities, it is important to prayerfully choose one and *only one* point for this particular homily. This discernment then leads to writing the focus and function statements, which will guide the construction of the homily and keep it unified.

Focus and Function Statements

Fred Craddock suggests that in the process of preparing a homily, the preacher is looking for two "eureka!" or "aha!" moments.[8] The first "aha!" is an event that is guided by the Holy Spirit. It results from prayerful and reflective discernment about the central message. Pondering the texts and reflecting on the nature and situation of those who will hear the homily, the preacher concludes, "Aha, this is what *I* must preach this Sunday from *this text* in these circumstances for *these people*."

Creating a focus and a function statement is an exercise in homiletic discernment as well as a spiritual discipline. If you know what you want to say and what you want the homily to do, you can craft and edit your way to a unified and cohesive homily.

Focus Statement:
What do you discern God wants to say/communicate?

- What do you want your people to think about and take home and into life in the next week?

- A focus statement grows from the text itself and is often a theological truth. Biblical texts both say and do something.

- It must be Good News. God, the Father, the Son, and/or the Holy Spirit should be the subject of the focus statement.

Function Statement:
What do I believe God wants to do in the hearer through this message?

- The biblical Word is not merely a message for the mind. The scriptures are endowed with power, with God's very presence.

- God seeks to transform us—that is an action at the heart of God's desire. Thus, pray and envision what that transformation in your hearers might look like.

- A function statement often *centers on a verb*; the transformation can be the deepening of something already present, an internal conversion of attitude or belief, or a resulting external change in behavior. It does not have to be a big change.

- Name that hoped-for change.

The focus and function statements should be related to each other. They should be clear, unified, and simple. Write them out and then edit them so they are straightforward. God is always the subject of the focus statement. Here's an example of struggling to create a coherent and unified focus statement:

Too general or vague:	**Multiple ideas or too ambitious or complex:**
God is love.	When we really truly know that we are loved by God and we get a sense of God's love in prayer, all we really want to do is to go and help the poor and change the world so that they can live a better life.

Strong focus statement:

God's love so transforms us that we want to reach out to others.

Form:
Structuring a Message and Creating a Logic of Movement

Often the potential impact of a homiletic message is diluted or obscured by a failure to attend to the need of the listener for a pathway by which to journey progressively into that message. One can make many good points in preaching, but if there is no coherent organization among them, the hearer's mind will not be able to grasp and retain them, and they will have little impact on the hearer's being or soul. Homiletic "form" or structure shapes the way the listener will hear, remember, and internalize the message. In other words, the structure carries a logic or thread of meaning. It organizes and conducts the hearer's attention, and shows the relationship between one section or homiletic "move" and the next. There is no one right structure, of course, but the choice of structure is not innocuous; it is worth careful discernment itself by the preacher.

Half Done

When you reach that moment of insight on what you think your homily must say and do, your preparation is only half done. A second insight is, "Aha, this is *how* I will get my message received." This second "aha" arises from further discernment, resulting in a decision about a way to present the message effectively for the listener to receive and act upon. Good preachers invest as much care in the second "aha" as in the first. You want your people to move with you through the homily. Thus you consciously arrange your pieces and parts into distinct *moves*. Then you fashion those moves into a deliberate form.

Deliberate Form

The purpose of creating a form is to help people to hear. You, as a preacher, consciously order the parts of the homily to smooth the path for active listening.

Thus, the structure of preaching—usually called homiletic *form*—must be carefully considered and deliberate. It is not so much a plan for what the preacher will say but rather "*a plan for the experience of listening.*"[9] The choice of form is guided by content and purpose. It must be congenial both to the gospel and to the ways people hear, receive, and appropriate important communication.

The Purposes of Form

Form is not incidental or neutral. It has at least five important goals:

1. It gains and holds interest.
2. It shapes the listener's experience of the material.
3. It shapes the listener's faith.
4. It shapes the degree and kind of participation demanded of the hearers.
5. It may facilitate a fresh hearing of the familiar.[10]

How you say what you have to say is as important as what you have to say.

Creating a Path for People to Follow

As you stand to preach, you are a leader among your people. This is a high calling, deserving your best efforts. As you have discerned the message that you believe God is calling you to speak, you seek to lead your people to God. You want them to hear that message as clearly as possible.

First, in prayer, you will have gathered ideas—you may have lots of them; you may not. Then you put all of those pieces together. What is your main claim, your focus, and your function? How will you structure your words so the homily moves and takes people somewhere?

Homiletic spiritual leadership prayerfully, slowly, and steadily stretches and challenges the flock of the faithful to climb the mountain of God. We invite them to re-envision their lives in the light of God's gracious and ongoing action. Only the Holy Spirit can touch the inner soul of our listeners. But as preachers, we can allow the Holy Spirit to help us continually learn how to bring that conversion about. With our people, we form an alliance of trust. We want to encounter God together. To accompany our people and to challenge them to come closer to Jesus Christ is homiletic spiritual leadership. That shepherding role is our mission in preaching.

Discuss and Reflect

1. When and in what ways have you experienced leadership through your preaching?

2. Think about a time, perhaps only a fleeting moment, when you felt as though you were leading and guiding your people as you were preaching. How was that different from other homiletic moments?

3. Look ahead to the "Try This" section and the "Read or View" suggestions below. Which of those do you discern as something to try or read or view that would help you to grow in your preaching abilities?

Try This!

1. *Be an attentive leader.* During the coming month, keep a journal or write notes below of things that you notice—fragmentary incidents, stray comments, close observations and descriptions of what you see, and your own thoughts that pop out of the blue. Be particularly mindful of two crucial dispositions for effective preaching: knowing yourself and knowing your people.

2. *Know yourself.* Communications experts say that the more you know of a subject, the less you can recall what it is like not to know it.[11] Thus the more theological training you have, the less you remember what it was like not to understand theology. Think back to the days before you were in seminary. How and where did you experience God? How did you name your experience of God at that time? How is your experience of God now different.

3. *Know your people.* To become more perceptive about where your people encounter God, first believe that they do. Expect that the Holy Spirit is at work in their lives, even if they do not name the Spirit explicitly. Then ask them where they encounter God. Ask them at pastoral council meetings, at parent meetings, at finance council meetings, and at youth group. Ask them after Sunday Masses or at one-on-one meetings. Ask broadly and take notes. Don't just ask your inner circle (who may use more "churchy language"), but ask at the times when you encounter those who are on the edges of faith—at baptismal meetings, marriage prep, and football games—questions such as these:

3a. *How do you experience God?* (Listen for the implicit ways in which they do *not* experience God.)

3b. *Where do you most find beauty, goodness, joy, or happiness?* What's the most beautiful thing you have ever seen?

4. Be an interviewer and do what Morgan Freeman did on the National Geographic series *The Story of God with Morgan Freeman*.[12] Ask, in your own context, "Do you believe in *miracles*? If so, tell me about that." Work to more fully incorporate what you notice and hear of your people's language and experiences into your homilies this month.

Read or View

Read or view additional materials found in this companion folder: https://bit.ly/RememberingWhyWePreach or use this code:

The materials for this chapter include the following:

Stephen Vincent DeLeers, "The Homily as Actualizing Word: Written Text becomes Living Word," chap. 8 in *Written Text Becomes Living Word: The Vision and Practice of Sunday Preaching*, 119–30 (Collegeville, MN: Liturgical Press, 2004).

J. Ronald Knott, "Claiming the Pulpit for Spiritual Leadership and Personal Sanctification," chap. 18 in *Preaching as Spiritual Leadership: Guiding the Faithful as Mystic and Mystagogue*, ed. Michael E. Connors, 177–85 (Chicago: Liturgy Training, 2021).

Sample homily by Pope John Paul II. All materials used with permission.

Suggested Reading for Further Study

Francis. Apostolic Exhortation *Evangelii Gaudium* (*The Joy of the Gospel*) 150–154. Washington, DC: US Conference of Catholic Bishops, 2013. On discernment and leadership.

Rahner, Karl. "The Holy Spirit and the Mysticism of Everyday Life." In *The Content of Faith: The Best of Karl Rahner's Theological Writings*, edited by Karl Lehmann and Albert Raffelt, 367–72. New York: Crossroad, 2014.

Taylor, Barbara Brown. "The Practice of Encountering Others." Chap. 6 in *An Altar in the World: A Geography of Faith*. New York: HarperOne, 2009.

Wallace, James A. "Preaching's Task in a New Millennium: Feeding God's People." Chap. 1 in *Preaching to the Hungers of the Heart: The Homily on the Feasts and within the Rites*, 1–27. Collegeville, MN: Liturgical Press, 2002.

6.

Opening the Conversation between Pulpit and Pew

Feedback from the pews reaps benefits for both listeners and preachers. How do we begin the conversation within our parishes so that we pastorally speak to our own hearers?

The Benefits of Feedback

It had been bugging him for four years: "Why does this man always close his eyes when I'm preaching?" Finally, the priest had enough. He went to the man in the second pew and asked, "Why do you always close your eyes when I'm preaching?" The man responded simple, "I listen better that way."

A bishop bemoaned that one of his earlier congregations sat like stones when he preached—no nods, no smiles, and no acknowledgment that he was getting through. Then he ran a survey. It turned out they were listening. They appreciated his words of wisdom. They were actually getting a lot out of his preaching. Who knew?

In most realms of life we get better at something by having constant rounds of feedback and coaching: writing, golf, playing a musical instrument, and handling parish finances; even in friendships and family relationships we get feedback about how we are relating. Yet seminary formation often encourages us to face upward toward our superiors for feedback, and not downward toward the people for insight. We need both. Deacon David Shea says, "Most of us tend to preach in a vacuum where we are forced to assess our own preaching and draw conclusions using the few tidbits of input that we only casually and informally receive. We preach without the benefit of concrete feedback that could make a radical difference in what and how we preach."[1]

There is a cultural silence with regard to feedback in most parish cultures. *Are* the people growing through our preaching? We hear them laugh, we see them nod, and we may instinctively analyze their moments of silence to determine when they have been touched by our words. They are already speaking back nonverbally, if we know how to read them and listen for what they are telling us. They are with us in that homiletic moment. Yet we don't definitively know how and when we are bringing our people into an encounter with God.

Bishop Kenneth Untener wrote that "good feedback is priceless because it can be hard to get."[2] How much good do we miss by not having this local conversation?

The discussion about preaching already takes place in the parking lots and at dinner tables. But people hold back about opening a mutually beneficial conversation about preaching. As one listener said, "But I couldn't talk about that to Father!" Many of us in our priestly ministry strive to be approachable and good listeners. But no matter how welcoming we may be, people do not automatically think we are interested in how they receive our preaching. We may have to intentionally let them know that we *want* their response.

As clergy, listening is an essential dimension of our lives. We listen to the sick in the hospital, we listen to the concerns of parents about their children, and we listen to engaged couples in marriage preparation. Since preaching is also a form of pastoral ministry, listening plays an important role here too. We seek to speak to our people's real needs and hungers. Our formation may have taught us "to get the Gospel said." At the same time, it is worth striving to put in the extra effort "to get the Gospel heard" in a way that truly connects with our people.[3] Our ministry will flourish as we witness those "aha!" moments among our listeners. Thus our homiletic growth will depend on listening.

How do we open a conversation in the local community—pulpit and pew together? This suggests a cultural shift. How do we go about creating that change?

Where to Start

First, start small. Start by asking. Bishop Untener carried a pocket notebook with him wherever he went. He asked "friends, strangers, at dinner tables, parties and on airplanes," what they liked and didn't like about homilies.[4] He found that people are certainly willing to talk about preaching! You can imitate those personal conversations by talking with men, women, and youth whom you respect. These conversations can occur informally one-on-one over a cup of coffee, sitting at a football game, at a baptismal party, or in nearly any other situation. Get as broad a sample as possible (not just those who affirm you at daily Mass). The goal is to just start asking. Then really listen and value what they say to you. If they know you are interested, people will talk.

Second, absorb spiritual insights and life experiences from groups you already interact with. Some parishes unpack the upcoming scriptures at pastoral council, committee and/or staff meetings. Others unpack what they heard and took to heart from the previous Sunday's Liturgy of the Word. You can alternate the varieties of lectio divina described in chapter 3 if you try something like this. Though communal lectio may lengthen a meeting, it helps you to be more in tune with what people are living through. It may also form them into more careful readers of scripture with the added potential to become better feedback givers. It may also help them to be more spiritually focused in their ministries. A leader in a large suburban parish enjoyed the input from his people in parish meetings:

> I ask that their prayer include one of the readings . . . that way, it sort of allows me to be a little bit more lazy (*much laughter*), because I can steal all the reflections from staff or from another meeting, in terms of what people are thinking about and how they are interacting with it. . . . So, instead of me just being alone in my room with a couple of books, you're getting, "What is the staff thinking about, related to this reading?" "How do they hear it?" "What are they getting out of it?"

Third, if they have been carefully selected, the most theologically trained laypeople you interact with are your staff members. They are near at hand, have much contact with parishioners, and can give you valuable insight. From a study of parish and diocesan lay leaders, they themselves suggested that the conversation would be best initiated by the preacher himself.[5] Because of the power dynamics surrounding employment, many staff members might be understandably reluctant to give feedback to their pastor. Feedback to an associate pastor who is not the boss may feel safer, depending on his personality and his relationships with the lay staff. Pastoral associates and directors of religious education (DREs) may be reticent to broach the topic of the homily, but they are grateful when asked. One woman said, "Pastors and deacons need to ask for input. I had one that did that and I think it helped."

Again, a greater measure of safety comes when the leader begins the conversation: one homilist checked in with his youth minister on Wednesdays as he was crafting his Sunday homily, asking, "What are the kids going through this week?"

In the days before First Communion, a one-on-one conversation with the DRE or with the sacramental preparation team may provide anecdotes and themes for the homily preached for that occasion. Initiating this kind of informal conversation sends a message that a response from the parish staff is welcome, especially when exegeting the congregation. Be a safe haven for them to give you input.

Fourth, moving further, in 1982, the US Catholic Bishops' document on preaching, *Fulfilled in Your Hearing*, suggested carefully structured preaching preparation and/or feedback groups that gather regularly in the week before the homily to unpack the scriptures together.[6] These groups could give feedback afterward as well. When creating parish preparation groups, it is most helpful to find someone to coordinate and convene them (who is not you, the preacher). You are then free to be a listener.

Fifth, parish surveys can be helpful in getting a finger on the pulse of a parish as well as help in assessing how the preaching is "landing" in the pews. When the survey is voluntary, your results will be skewed in favor of those who are willing to give you feedback. This can create an artificially positive or negative response. Yet even that can be beneficial. Again, try to get as broad a sample as possible. Examples for surveys can be found in the "Try This" section of this chapter.

Opening yourself to homiletic feedback from the pews can leave you feeling vulnerable. It does carry risks, both for you and for the giver. Some feedback may miss the mark or be theologically uninformed. They may tell you that they like your jokes. They might like your friendly manner. They may not have high expectations for the homily from past experience, so they are simply happy that you do not offend them. They may not understand that the purpose of the homily is to lead them to God.

Understanding those limitations, we listen anyway. This imperfection may also offer an opportunity to educate our people more deeply about the Catholic understanding of preaching. A rich adult education program could be built around a reading and discussion of *Fulfilled in Your Hearing*.[7] Deeper understanding of what we are seeking in preaching not only would improve the quality of homiletic feedback but also could sharpen people's eagerness to listen, helping them become active participants rather than passive recipients.

Using Feedback to Grow

If you are meeting with a peer learning group to study these materials and evaluate each other's homilies or you have found a personal preaching coach, you may have started getting feedback on your preaching. How will you grow from that?

Getting too little feedback can give you a skewed idea of how you are doing: no words of encouragement from the pew can make you feel as if your preaching is doing no good at all. "Great homily!" can swell your head so you perceive yourself as better than you really are—you may not feel you need to improve because you are already pretty darn good. We have seen both attitudes in our coaching experiences.

Douglas Stone and Sheila Heen suggest that the challenge to long-term effectiveness is in how you respond to feedback. How carefully do you receive and implement the feedback you receive? How focused are you on continuing to learn? Your personal coachability and your willingness to act on feedback will affect how much you will grow from those experiences.[8]

Internal mental processing can make us resist feedback. We may say to ourselves, (1) They're wrong—I'm actually better than they say, or (2) Wow, I must really be a schmuck, not any good at all. Both the artificially self-aggrandizing and the self-deprecatingly negative responses block growth. To humbly respond to feedback, we can view ourselves with more complexity—none of us are totally excellent or thoroughly worthless.[9] There are ways in which we could grow. If we see our homiletic skills as a mixture of strengths and flaws, we will continue to train our weaknesses and preach from our strengths.

At this point in this process of renewal, getting too much feedback can actually discourage you. Now that you know where the homily is intended to go, you may have set a higher bar for yourself and your preaching, and you may not yet know how to succeed in achieving those goals. If you don't already have one, this would be a good time to get a trained homiletics coach to help you move forward.

Initiating Congregational Assessment

In the "Try This" section of this chapter, we begin congregational assessment. Your response to feedback from your parishioners will influence the comfort level with which they will continue to give it to you. One of our ideals for this process is for you to establish ongoing feedback in your parish so you continue to flourish in your preaching ministry. You may be surprised to learn how much impact your seven- to ten-minute weekly homily has in the lives of your people. Bishop Untener found his people quite loquacious: "Surprising how willing people were (and are) to talk about [preaching]."[10] When you consciously foster the local relationship on preaching, you create a cultural shift so that preaching becomes an act of love within a milieu of caring: "Those who listen will love those who preach. Those who preach will love those who listen."[11]

Discuss and Reflect

1. Reflect on your reactions to this chapter's invitation to actively seek out homiletic feedback from your hearers. What does it stir within you? An eagerness to hear from usually silent parishioners? Hesitation? Or even resistance? A bit of fear, perhaps borne of the apprehension that "I'm not good enough," or arising from a bruising experience of feedback in seminary formation or a job? Identify the sources of your reactions.

2. Think of a time when one of your listeners gave you an unexpected bit of affirmation or challenge to something you said in a homily. Was the feedback put in a constructive way? How so, or how not so? How would you describe the kind of feedback you would find helpful to your growth as a preacher?

3. Challenge yourself this week to listen deeply and carefully to at least three people. What did you hear? What did it take for you to really listen? What was the effect on the other?

Try This!

This month, try one type of congregational feedback. According to Stone and Heen, feedback comes in three types: appreciation, coaching, and evaluation. Evaluation can drown out the other two, though all coaching includes some evaluation. Determine which of the following three you could do. What response do you need? What would help your parish the most? The three examples that follow are designed to elicit listener response for the three types of feedback.

Appreciation

The purpose of appreciation is to motivate and encourage. A simple homily feedback postcard is placed in the pew and offers two questions. In your introductory remarks, mention the card in the pew and that you'd like a wide range of people to fill it out. Ask your people to be especially attentive to how God might be speaking to them personally through the words of the homily (this tends to make them listen more carefully).

Take a few moments *after the homily* to allow people to fill it out, and then at the offertory, have them drop it in the basket. Hopefully, these postcards will (a) help you see that God is speaking through your preaching and (b) encourage your listeners to be listening for what God is doing in their lives. If you find that your hearers' responses are all over the place as they report on what they heard, the variation might suggest that you need to tune your focus a little more tightly. (Some variation is normal and to be expected.) Try it once a month for several months and see what happens.

 Homily Feedback Card

This is what I heard as the main point of the homily:

This is what I felt that God was saying to me through it:

Please fill this card out and drop it in the collection basket. *Thank you!*

Coaching

Ask for listener response in the bulletin or select a few people to give you this feedback. You can also assign different members of a preaching preparation team to give you the "after-homily" response. You are looking to be coached in what is "sticky" in your preaching—what is memorable and how that memory helps your people to continue to encounter God.

Electronic Feedback (3-4 days later)	Verbal or Written Feedback (1 week later)
Here is what I remember from what you said on Sunday:	Here is what I took away from what you said last Sunday:
This is why I remember it:	This is how I let it affect my life this
This is how that memory has helped me in the last three days:	

Evaluation

Congregational assessment can be designed in a more comprehensive way to evaluate the strengths and weaknesses of several preachers. We give a very basic example here. To understand results, you might want to enlist the help of a parishioner who is skilled in data analysis. Representative sampling can be a challenge; instead of putting these surveys out for anyone to voluntarily respond, perhaps choose five to eight groups in the parish and have each person fill it out in a ten-minute space. A cluster sample of the youth group, the Knights of Columbus, the Altar and Rosary Society, the school parents' group, and a social justice group might give you a variety of involved people. Specify that they are to evaluate the homily and the homilist that they heard the last time they went to Mass (so they don't select their favorite).

The Sunday Homily I Last Heard   *Name of Homilist*_____

Please circle the number that gives your most accurate response to the Sunday homily you last heard.	Strongly disagree	Disagree	Somewhat disagree	Neither	Somewhat agree	Agree	Strongly agree
1. The Sunday homily made me feel full of life.	1	2	3	4	5	6	7
2. The homily had a central idea that I can still remember.	1	2	3	4	5	6	7
3. The homily used words, examples, and images I can relate to.	1	2	3	4	5	6	7
4. Through that homily, I deepened my relationship with God/Jesus Christ/the Holy Spirit.	1	2	3	4	5	6	7
5. The homily helped me in the struggles of daily life.	1	2	3	4	5	6	7
6. The homily spurred me to do something to be more like Jesus.	1	2	3	4	5	6	7
7. The homily spoke to me personally.	1	2	3	4	5	6	7
8. The homily helped me to understand the scriptures better.	1	2	3	4	5	6	7
9. The homily opened my heart to be better disposed to receive the Eucharist.	1	2	3	4	5	6	7
10. The homily inspired a positive discussion with my family and friend(s).	1	2	3	4	5	6	7
11. If I had a video or a written copy of this homily, or a link to it on the web, I would recommend it or give it to a friend.	1	2	3	4	5	6	7

Read or View

Read or view additional materials found in this companion folder: https://bit.ly/RememberingWhyWePreach or use this code:

    The materials for this chapter include the following:

Karla J. Bellinger, *Connecting Pulpit and Pew: Breaking Open the Conversation about Catholic Preaching* (Collegeville, MN: Liturgical Press, 2014), epilogue, 145.

Kenneth Untener, *Preaching Better* (New York: Paulist Press, 1999), chap. 19, 98–101.

Bishops' Committee on Priestly Life and Ministry, *Fulfilled in Your Hearing: The Homily in the Sunday Assembly* (Washington, DC: US Conference of Catholic Bishops, 1982), 36–38. All materials used with permission.

Suggested Reading for Further Study

Harris, Daniel E. *We Speak the Word of the Lord: A Practical Plan for More Effective Preaching.* Chicago: ACTA Publications, 2001.

- Fr. Dan offers practical suggestions for organizing a preaching discussion group on pages 184–91. This is a good book to have on the preaching shelf.

Stone, Douglas, and Sheila Heen. *Thanks for the Feedback: The Science and Art of Receiving Feedback Well.* New York: Viking, 2014.

- This book by the authors of the best-selling book Difficult Conversations: How to Discuss What Matters Most, expands on one element of a difficult conversation: the reception of feedback. What helps us to hear others well? What blocks us, triggers our anger or resistance, or keeps us from growing from the feedback of others? Even when read only in snatches, this book is beneficial for preachers.

7.

Moving through Encounter to Discipleship

Knowing Jesus Christ by faith is our joy; following him is a grace, and passing on this treasure to others is a task entrusted to us by the Lord, in calling and choosing us.[1]

The Centrality of Preaching for Encounter

In the last six chapters, we have looked at falling in love with Jesus Christ. We have explored what brings our people closer to God. And we have studied what preaching for encounter means for the ways we preach. Yet as each of us has recognized, we cannot control a person's inner experience. It is the Spirit of God who ignites that "aha!" moment. But there are ways of preaching that make an encounter with the living God more likely to happen. Before we move forward, let us recap what that may have looked like in your preaching.

As you yourself deepened in your spiritual life, the Holy Spirit has spoken through you more clearly. Perhaps you have had some of the following experiences. Forlorn and feeling alone, a woman's eyes filled with tears as you spoke of a God who travels to the ends of the world to show his love for her. Your gentle words, "God is here with us,

God is here with you, do not be afraid," gave a boost to a discouraged working man. You named the Paschal Mystery: in the midst of human darkness, you spoke of the One who brings us light. You supported the young mother who struggles to get four little children to Mass. You listened. You prayed about what to preach. You discerned. You saw a man who was jaded about life, who wondered whether there was any point to going on—you challenged him to the adventure of the Gospel, to be one of God's heroes who works for the good of the world in which he lives, and he swelled with courage. You upheld the saints in your pews, you affirmed the ways in which they sacrifice and serve, and you gave them strength to carry on. With preaching as an act of love, of caring, with an intentional pastoral focus, Jesus Christ has been speaking through you to comfort the challenged and challenge the comfortable. Thank you for your good work!

As you have made a conscious effort to throw your shoulder into preaching for encounter, you have brought the living God close. It is a privilege to offer words that reveal the nearness of God. Joy "comes from the *closeness of God*, from his *presence* in our lives."[2] We hope that sharing that closeness has been your joy and your delight. So where do we go next?

Moving to Discipleship

The bishops of Latin America, in their Aparecida statement quoted at the beginning of this chapter, move from "*knowing* Jesus Christ" to *following* him. We would like to make that same move as we travel through this process together. We have focused on bringing our people into an encounter with the living God. Now we step forward to explore these further questions: How do we nourish the fruit that an encounter with God bears? How do we preach to move our people from that initial encounter into deeper discipleship?

A parallel can be found with falling in love. In a romantic relationship, love leads two people to give themselves to each other in the commitment of marriage. Similarly, in our faith relationship with Christ, it is love that spurs us to give ourselves to him. Over the long haul, both to keep a marriage faithfully together and to follow Jesus requires two things: (1) continually renewing that love and (2) committing to the relationship on an ongoing basis.

We know we cannot make that commitment on our own. God's grace is the source of all discipleship. God first draws close to us (*CCC*, 1). Dietrich Bonhoeffer says, "Discipleship is not an offer man makes to Christ."[3] The initiative is always God's. The Spirit of God calls us, captivates us, and entices us. There was something deeply alluring about the person of Jesus of Nazareth. The Gospel of Mark tells us, "People kept coming to him from everywhere" (Mk 1:45). People wanted to be near him. They wanted to touch him. They wanted to hear him. They came by night. They came by day. "Follow me" was his appealing invitation. As with his earliest disciples, he calls us to drop our nets and come along in his company, to live as he lived, to do as he did. That is discipleship.

As Catholics, we may recoil from promoting "a personal commitment to Jesus Christ." It sounds a little too arm-twistingly evangelical Protestant. Yet Catholics have long committed themselves to God: popular devotions have encouraged "consecration" to the Sacred Heart and to Mary. Aspirations and ejaculations are short prayers of faithfulness taught to be repeated throughout the day. The morning (or daily) offering is a consecration for that day, a conscious and willing decision to dedicate one's soul, mind, heart, and body to God. The "amen" when receiving the Body of Christ is our Eucharistic "yes!" However we name it, we Catholics *do* respond with yes. That word of continual invitation is "a gift before it is a challenge" (*Evangelii Gaudium* 142). We are not born again once. We respond with a daily, committed, and ongoing yes to the Lord who says, "Follow me!"

Thus we are no longer our own; we belong to God. At the core of discipleship, within this full-throated yes, we model our very being after the personhood of Jesus. Just like the Son, we are to richly embrace the intimacy of his relationship with his "Abba" as beloved sons and daughters of God our Father. We are called to be like Jesus.

How do we follow? In many ways: we follow in the footsteps of the saints; we are to be willing to go wherever the Lord leads; we are to be neighbor, forgiver, and healer; we worship and witness; and we empty ourselves to be willing to suffer as Jesus suffered.[4] A disciple is to be steward and prophet, lover and self-giver, one who allows the Spirit to purify him or her into a life of holiness. Following Jesus is a grand adventure of challenge and joy at the same time. To be loved with an unfathomable love, to have Someone to call on when all seems lost, to live a vibrant and abundant life—how could we *not* want a life like that? No matter the cross, let us not be afraid to preach the expansive joy of discipleship. If we do not, it is as though we are holding back the greatest of gifts, like keeping gold in your pocket while a pauper stands before you pleading for a penny.

Preaching that Urges Our People toward Discipleship

So then, what does it mean to preach in order to move our people from encounter to discipleship? What do we need to get there?

Start with Ourselves

First, as we pray with scripture, we see a consistency in the way Jesus began his relationship with his disciples: he called them. With other teachers of his time, the students picked the master. Not this time. Jesus called his own followers. He wanted them. He selected them. In our preaching preparation, as we pray with the stories of Jesus, we come to our scriptural study with that eyesight of "being wanted" and "being called," with its accompanying call to conversion. Fr. Mike Fones, OP, describes that shift in his own eyesight: "My preaching has changed over the last few years. I am surprised by how often the scriptures give me an opportunity to preach on conversion, on the meaning of the cross, on what it means to be a disciple of Jesus. . . . My previous bias, which did not take life-changing conversion seriously, gave me 'eyes that did not see' and 'ears that did not hear' what I now see and hear so clearly."[5]

Carefully Work the Content

When our eyesight changes, the content of our preaching will also change. We want to portray the Lord as he is: so appealing in his love and compassion that people will want to say yes. We will tell stories and paint pictures that don't just tell but also show that "you are wanted," "you are called," and "you are selected." We will preach consistently about the encounter that leads to discipleship. We will ask for courage, repentance, conversion of life, reaching out in mercy, offering forgiveness, and more. As we move from encounter to discipleship, we urge, plead, and show the way to respond. We preach "Come! Follow me!" in many and varied ways. Let us not be afraid to invite people onto the spiritual journey.

Address Pushback

In his day, not everyone was convinced to follow Jesus. Some hesitated. Some turned away and did not follow. From last month's listening to your listeners, you may have gained some sense of your own people's stumbling blocks. Until we address those hesitations in our preaching,[6] we will get nowhere in calling our people to discipleship.

When I (Karla) was a pastoral associate in a parish, I had a conversation with a woman who came to Mass only once in a while. She said, "Karla, when you say God loves us, I believe God loves you. I do. I believe that *you* believe God loves me." She shrugged, "*I* just don't believe that God loves *me*."

Discipleship relies on a sense of being wanted, loved deeply and personally. Many people in the pew, like this friend, may just not feel called.[7] Those who work in the Church (both clergy and lay) often have a strong sense that God has called them to do what they do every day. But for those who are not involved in parish activities, they may not see what they do with their time as a calling. It is just a job. It is a way to get by, a way to survive and put food on the table. How do we preach to that? Spiritual leadership means understanding the causes of pushback against committed discipleship. Then we pray and discern how to speak to those issues and attitudes.

Resistances to discipleship come in many forms. In Christian Smith's study of religion and youth and their parents, he found that the prevailing belief in the United States is what he termed *moralistic therapeutic deism* (MTD), the belief that God is a Divine Butler who is useful in times of trouble, comes when we call, is too nice to judge anyone, and asks us to be nicer people.[8] From Karla's empirical findings, much Catholic preaching leans toward MTD; our preaching tends to ask us to be nicer people without much mention of following Jesus and the grace that undergirds that following.[9] Yet Mass-attending youth themselves asked for their preachers to go deeper. How do we do that? How do we foster the awareness that we depend on God, that we need the Lord's help? How can we choreograph moments of silence where God can speak to our people?

In laying out the challenge to follow Jesus, we have to address the pushback and the resistances. How can we dissolve the illusion of self-sufficiency? How do we preach to a reductionism that diminishes the God of Christianity to one deity (often among many other options) who is merely useful to our ends? (This chapter's "Try This" section gives concrete examples to help you do that.)

Put Words to the Good News

How do we find the words and stories to make that appeal persuasive? Notice how our culture gives us many words for cynicism and bad news. Where do we find words to illumine the good? We can use the words of liturgical prayers, the lyrics of songs and hymns, images of religious art, and metaphors of the spiritual masters. We have stories of saints and role models in everyday people who followed Jesus in their own walks of life. To preach an encounter that leads to unswerving discipleship, we pull from all of those sources.

Delivery

We don't have photographs of what Jesus looked like. Many paintings of him are cheerless. Yes, discipleship requires sacrifice. Carrying the cross is integral to following our Master. At the same time, we are people of hope. We are people who "clearly live and witness to the fact that the Jesus who *was* is also a Jesus who *is*."[10] If we are filled with a sense of resurrection, it will show. "A cheerful face and eyes full of joy . . . these are signs that we're following this path of all or nothing, of fullness emptied out," Pope Francis says.[11] We reveal with our faces and our bodies that we are excited about the Good News. As a personal witness to the Gospel, we don't just talk; we embody that invitation to meet the One who is at the center of our own lives. Our demeanor takes on a new urgency—we *show* that this Jesus stuff matters to us.

Disciples beget disciples.[12] That is why we spent the first half of our process on our own renewal as preachers. Two seconds of loving eye contact, a smile of joy, and arms and a face that moves with enthusiasm and love of God—the appeal of Christian discipleship is as much caught as taught.

Preach to Build Community

Since faith is caught, we also preach to build a community that supports discipleship. To follow Jesus, we need the incarnational support of flesh-and-blood people. The carpenter from Nazareth worked with a group of disciples. In the same way, none of us are called to walk alone. Preaching plays a part in building community by fostering a sense of "us," using the plural "you and me" in naming the faith of the local community. William E. Simon says, "Discipleship is the central focus of vibrant parishes."[13] The parish is to be a home base, a place to be strengthened and built up in our Christian life. Yet the parish is not the end point of discipleship. Disciples are called out into the world.

Ask

If we want committed discipleship, we have to ask for it. Jesus did. We are sometimes too timid to ask, which is really a neglect of the will in the mind/heart/will triad. There are ways to express this that are not too reminiscent of an altar call and that avoid moralism and Pelagianism. Commitment to Jesus grows more solid when we move beyond the interiority of mind and heart and do something public and active, which gets our feet and hands and personal budgets in the game. We can show examples of people who take the plunge, cast aside fear, and make Christ the center of their lives. We can ask people to come to the sacraments more often, set aside time for prayer, engage in public witness to the faith, serve a neglected neighbor, and share with a spouse or friend that you'd like to make your faith a higher priority. Yes, our preaching can be that direct when it is delivered with love and in joy.

We are all called to be followers of Jesus. Since the homily is integral to liturgy, those seven to ten minutes of words from the ambo lead us to God and to the table. Then together as a community, fueled by both Word and sacrament, we go out to be light to the world. What could be more joyous than that?

Discuss and Reflect

1. Retrace your own journey of faith. What people and practices nudged you toward a life of more serious commitment to following Jesus? How might you incorporate these things into your preaching and pastoral practice?

2. Dietrich Bonhoeffer and others have spoken of discipleship's "cost."[14] What has following Jesus cost you? What has the cost been in the lives of others you have observed? How might you speak of this in preaching?

3. How do you call your hearers to discipleship, to deeper commitment to God, or to holiness? How have you observed other preachers doing so effectively and in ways that have brought others to Christ?

Try This!

In the chart below are anonymous comments from undergraduate students in response to the question "Why do you resist God and prayer?" The question followed an experiment: Each student was given two magnets to hold half an inch away from each other. We discussed how the internal *pull* of God feels, how gentle that attraction feels, and how easy it is to miss that tug. Then we turned one of the magnets around and felt the two magnets pushing against each other, recognizing how our resistances are also small and how easy they are to miss. In that context, the students described the following attitudes and perspectives that caused them to resist God and prayer.

Try this magnet experiment with your selected group of responders. Give them a chance to feel both the attraction and the resistance. Then ask them that same question: "Why do you resist God and prayer?" This may give you fodder for preaching. For your next homily, adapt one of the responses below or use a response from your parish to use as a springboard in discerning your focus (What do I want this homily to say?) and function (What do I want this homily to do?) statements.

Why I resist God and prayer	What scriptures, words, quotes, and stories could I use if I were to speak to that resistance?
I cannot see myself as the person God calls me to be–I am not worthy enough to have that relationship.	
Selfishness in my busy day-to-day life and being too caught up in myself pulls me farther away from God.	
Distractions and mindlessness makes me forget about God. My commitments keep me away from God. I try to do everything. God is just one among many things in my life.	
When I let people in, I get burned; I feel the same way about God. Multiple bad things happening in my life pulls me away from God. Perceived injustices, perceived abandonments that are thorns in the heart, and a mist between God and my soul.	
My false belief that I am master of my own universe makes me feel autonomous, fully in control of my day-to-day existence. Sometimes I value my independence more than my belief in, love of, and dependence on God.	

Why I resist God and prayer (continued)	What scriptures, words, quotes, and stories could I use if I were to speak to that thought?
I find it hard to give up control and my worries to put complete faith in anything, including God; the only person I can trust is myself.	
Sometimes God feels like a chore, like another thing on my to-do list. I don't see immediate gain.	
Fear—I fear that God will ask of me what I cannot give—I fear that opening myself and trusting will lead to something unendurable; this fear comes from old wounds.	
What causes me to resist God is being around people of little faith. A lot of my close friends don't believe in God or don't really prioritize God in their lives, and I want to keep their respect.	
The "milieu Christianity"—people professing a faith but not really living it.	
I resist (God) because you can't prove it. You can't prove these ideas are fake either. That uncertainty makes me hesitant to pick one side. Frankly, to me, it's not about picking a side. It's about living well.	

Read or View

Read or view additional materials found in this companion folder: https://bit.ly/RememberingWhyWePreach or use this code:

The materials for this chapter include the following:

Hannah Brockhaus, "Pope Francis in Colombia: True Freedom Is Found in Courageous Discipleship," Catholic News Agency, September 9, 2017, https://www.catholicnewsagency.com.

Michael E. Connors, "Preaching for Discipleship," chap. 10 in *Preaching for Discipleship: Preparing Homilies for Christian Initiation*, 161–79 (Chicago: Liturgy Training Publications, 2018).

A video clip of part of a talk by Pope Francis. All materials used with permission.

Suggested Reading for Further Study

Schmitz, Mike. "Discipleship 101: Free to Obey." UMD Newman, February 11, 2018,
    https://bulldogcatholic.org.

Williams, Oliver F. "Baptismal Witness in the World of Commerce." Chap. 12 in
    What We Have Seen and Heard: Fostering Baptismal Witness in the World, edited
    by Michael E. Connors, 165–78. Eugene, OR: Wipf and Stock, 2017.

8.

Preaching to Move Disciples into Mission

Every Christian is a missionary to the extent that he or she has encountered the love of God in Christ Jesus: We no longer say that we are "disciples" and "missionaries" but rather that we are always "missionary disciples." (*Evangelii Gaudium* 120)

The Mission of the Laity

Jesus said, "Come after me, and I will make you fishers of men" (Mt 4:19). When we go fishing as followers of Jesus, where do we go? A young person might feel, "If I am called to be holy, then I should become a priest, a religious sister, or a lay ecclesial minister; I could be a lector or a deacon or join a bible study." One temptation when we begin to talk about "following Jesus" is to think of disciples as solely a churchy cast. As parish leaders, we are too often tempted to ask, "If you want to follow Jesus, how can you get more involved in your parish?" But is getting people involved in the parish our ultimate goal? The parish is not the endpoint of discipleship. So, where *are* the laity called to live out their faith?

In the Second Vatican Council, one major development was to recognize that the baptized are called to holiness in the world *in which they live*.[1] Therefore *the Church is missionary by its very nature*;[2] it has one mission, the mission of Christ, which is lived out in many and various ways in our world.[3] The parish is the place to be strengthened and nourished so that laypeople can go out to all the world! Do our people know that?

I (Karla) was having a conversation with a well-educated Catholic layman. He asked what I was currently working on in my writing. I said, "Preaching for Mission." His eyes lit up; his response was immediate: "You should go talk to Father M., he spent a lot of time in Bangladesh!" I had to smile. Mission: the word evokes exotic places, difficult circumstances heroically overcome, and visiting priests telling stories of the hungry and the helpless. Many lay Catholics still interpret "mission" as something someone else does somewhere else. Mission is for missionaries, and lay Catholics are expected to give money to "the missions."

But what truly is the mission of the laity? What are laypeople called to do? The Second Vatican Council viewed the laity as full participants in the Church's divine mission; we are *all* Church. Full participation in the life of the Church, for the laity, is primarily through engagement with the world:

> But the laity, by their very vocation, seek the kingdom of God by engaging in temporal affairs and by ordering them according to the plan of God. They live in the world, that is, in each and in all of the secular professions and occupations. They live in the ordinary circumstances of family and social life, from which the very web of their existence is woven. They are called there by God that by exercising their proper function and led by the spirit of the Gospel they may work for the sanctification of the world from within as a leaven. In this way they may make Christ known to others, especially by the testimony of a life resplendent in faith, hope and charity. Therefore, since they are tightly bound up in all types of temporal affairs, it is their special task to order and to throw light upon these affairs in such a way that they may come into being and then continually increase according to Christ to the praise of the Creator and the Redeemer. (*Lumen Gentium* 31)[4]

Continuing this teaching, Pope Francis appeals for all of the faithful to be "missionary disciples" wherever we find ourselves. We fall in love with Jesus Christ. We are empowered by the Holy Spirit. As a result, daily life can no longer remain the same. Whether fishermen or computer programmers, preachers or lay ministers, parents or grandparents, when we encounter the friendship of God, all of us as the baptized are called to radiate that divine love. We show forth that passion, each in the ordinary moments of everyday life in our own particular ways. That is our calling. By God's grace, the world will be transformed through such action. And so will we.

Mission is dynamic. That dynamism arises from the Trinitarian God who both *is* mission and *has* a mission—to be a gift of love. The Church takes part in that mission as a sacrament of that Trinitarian love to the world. Building from the last unit, discipleship is not an isolated decision that remains within a parish building. Discipleship is a way of life, taking part in God's mission to go out and transform the world. Interior commitment and focus are part of an exterior life of mission. To be a disciple, then, is to have a purpose: to work for God's reign.

Pope Francis continually challenges the Church to "go out!" We are to be a community that is "permanently in a state of mission" (*Evangelii Gaudium* 25). We "go out" to the homes, the streets, and the workplaces. We "go out" on the subway, through recreation, and in prisons, nursing homes, and schools. We "go out" to be a gift of God's love to whomever we meet. St. John Paul II said, "The witness of a Christian life is the first and irreplaceable form of mission" (*Redemptoris Missio* 42).

All Christians are called to share the faith with joy, for "the entire people of God proclaims the Gospel" (*Evangelii Gaudium* 111). Jesus entrusted this evangelization to all of his followers. Thus as preachers, to repeat what we said in the introduction, our goal is to preach on Sunday so that our people will preach with their words and their actions on Monday—and beyond.[5]

Preaching to Move People toward Mission

So how do we as preachers speak so that we move our folks from encounter to discipleship to mission? The layman who suggested I talk to the missionary priest about missions did not see that he himself has a mission. The understanding of mission as something someone else does somewhere else keeps his personal calling at a distance. Many of our people in our pews live within that same mindset. So how do we strengthen and recast the vision of mission through our preaching?

Understand Their Mindset

Each parish culture is different. To begin to move *your* people toward mission, discern their strengths and look for their blind spots. You can gather that discernment from the preaching preparation groups you have formed or through informal conversation. Determine your people's understanding and practices of mission. Ask within your inner circle, ask those who sporadically attend Mass, and ask the youth at your parish. As you listen, you will see where you need to clarify and reeducate. Listen again and again. Know your people and know how they currently understand mission.

Preach a Sense of Purpose

When you preach, use synonyms and images for mission to help your people better picture that call. For instance, embracing the vision to be light and love to this world instills a sense of purpose and a reason for living. It has been said, "The two most important days in your life are the day you are born and the day that you find out why."[6] Realizing their mission offers to our people that why.

Pope Francis suggests that we don't just have a mission but that each of us *is* a mission. It is to embody that mission, he emphasizes, that we are alive. As he says,

> My mission of being in the heart of the people is not just a part of my life or a badge I can take off; it is not an "extra" or just another moment in life. Instead, it is something I cannot uproot from my being without destroying my very self. I am a mission on this earth; that is the reason why I am here in this world. We have to regard ourselves as sealed, even branded, by this mission of bringing light, blessing, enlivening, raising up, healing and freeing. (*Evangelii Gaudium* 273)

We are to be a gift of love to the world in which we live. We do this through service to others and by bearing witness to the living Christ whom we have met. Researchers tell us that a personal sense of purpose leads to greater personal well-being; thus, a great gift we can give to our parish and to those around us is to be a people of determination, resolution, drive, tenacity, and commitment to Jesus's way of life. How do we do that?

Fire Up the People for Mission

Laypersons are to play a leading part in transforming the world. No one else can do it as they can—it is the unique "duty and responsibility of the laity" (*Apostolicam Actuositatem* 13)—not the clergy, not the bishop—no one but them. *All* of us integral to the mission of the Church. Can we preach that? Our people know the darkness of the world in which they live. Do they know that *they*, by the grace of God, are to be the light, that they as "missionary disciples are little stars that mirror God's light?"[7] Living the Gospel is not to remain a private matter but rather to flourish in genuine love of neighbor that transforms all of society. In our preaching, we can fire them up by letting them know how crucial their living of the faith is, that *their* best efforts are needed.

In addition, we can both (1) affirm the value of their work and (2) orient (or reorient) that work toward larger purposes for the world and human living. Pope Francis did just that: he praised the work of nurses and urged them to "touch the sick like Jesus."[8]

He has celebrated Mass for gardeners and janitors; he consistently affirms them and urges them to follow Jesus in the ordinary jobs they do.

Many of our people may not feel called to the Church's mission, yet we can share with them that the Christian way of being is in not so much *what* they do but *how* they do it—how they move toward being a witness to the Gospel in their everyday lives. Relationships matter. "Man is more precious for who he is, rather than for what he does" (*Gaudium et Spes* 35). Many can be encouraged toward a purpose-driven life in the workplace.[9] Every Christian has a vocation, not just a job. The world needs honorable accountants, caring teachers, friendly gas station attendants, and joyful cashiers. The purpose of the Christian life is to be God's gift of love to the particular world in which they live.[10] That sense of "bloom where you're planted" is both call and mission.

Pope Francis seems to never stop talking about the relationship between encounter, discipleship, and mission. If we look at a list of the topics of his homilies, he constantly speaks to mission as our way of being in the world—he speaks of how to be in intimate relationship: with mercy and tenderness, through the look in our eyes, in our solidarity with the suffering, and by accompanying those close to us.

He is also not afraid to speak to the larger issues of our way of being in the world in regard to the poor, the outcast, those on the margins, refugees, and the powerless. This is his consistent homiletic theme: how to be a follower of Jesus in this world. In our own preaching, we can imitate that. We can affirm the small and local things— the love expressed in eye contact with a teenager, the tender touch on the arm of an elderly aunt, the smell of grandma's chocolate cake. We can unpack the social teaching of the Church in respecting the dignity of each human person—through work in food pantries, writing letters to legislators, and feeding the hungry in our midst. In our preaching, we can consistently remind our hearers that all of our actions, both large and small, are to be undertaken in a manner consistent with the furtherance of the kingdom of God.

Cautions

As you work on concretizing mission in everyday life through your preaching, we offer three cautions. First, we have to be cautious about messaging that simply reduces the Good News to morality. The Good News is so much more! It is a relationship with the divine that empowers self-sacrificing, loving, moral behavior. In some cultures, listeners expect to be told what to do, or even scolded from the pulpit. Yet as one in a position of authority, we want to preach for our adults to flourish as adults, not keep them dependent like children. So we need to be careful not to misdirect that pulpit authority.

Second, we can preach toward a virtuous way of life, but at the same time, we need to avoid Pelagianism. We do this by preaching often about the One who gives us *the power* to accomplish our mission. We cannot live a life of self-sacrifice all by ourselves. We cannot earn our salvation by our works. At all times, we are dependent on the power of the Spirit. The Holy Trinity—Father, Son, and Holy Spirit—is always the source, the help, and the goal of mission. In our individualistic culture, we can be tempted by pride, to become "do-gooders," relying on our own steam. It is essential to continually preach vulnerability, surrender, and reliance upon Almighty God as we do good works. We cannot walk this walk alone. God does not need our help, but he generously empowers us to participate in his saving work.

Third, if we are to move away from mission as "something someone else does somewhere else," we as the ordained must be cautious about speaking as though the secular world *is* somewhere else. We all live and serve in the same temporal world. It is a world at the same time beautiful and broken, graced and marred by sin. It can be revelatory of God as well. With our words, therefore, we need to be careful to speak of the secular world as a place to be honored, especially in the role of family, the dignity of work, and the value of ordinary life. Our respect (or lack of respect) leaks into our preaching. People can smell disregard. They also recognize the odor of one who reverences their lives and their world. They are grateful for that!

Constancy in Preaching for Mission

For long-term change of a parish culture, the vision of discipleship and mission needs to be preached over and over again, through scripture, story, metaphor, affirmation, and challenge. Say it in many and varied ways. Be constant. Look at the numerous ways that Pope Francis says, Follow Jesus! Be a person of mercy! Accompany! Befriend! Go to the peripheries! It is okay to repeat that theme continuously; just say it in different ways. As always, affirm where you see light. Assure your hearers that a life of generous service can be a life of joy. Lift up faith stories of laypeople who have lived lives of faith in ordinary circumstances. Affirm and imagine. In moving a parish from maintenance to mission, Fr. James Mallon suggests to capture the imagination by inviting parishioners to "dream the dream" by beginning with the word *imagine*: "Imagine if this was a parish that became a place where everyone was loved and accepted. . . . Imagine how our community and city would be transformed if our parish did. . . ."[11] Repeated envisioning keeps the dream front and center. What could *you* imagine in your parish? Invite your hearers to dream with you, for such dreams are the stuff of transforming action.

Your own excitement and enthusiasm for mission can be contagious. When you are on fire, you will embody the passion to pass on that fire. Good preaching is as much showing as telling. Be *always* on the lookout for inspiring stories, metaphors, examples, saints (local if possible), and missionary discipleship as a way of life right here in this locale. Look at the (very preachable) image-laden words that Pope Francis uses to illumine how encounter and mission are as much caught as taught: "Those who have opened their hearts to God's love, heard his voice and received his light, cannot keep this gift to themselves. . . . Faith is passed on, we might say, by contact, from one person to another, just as one candle is lighted from another" (*Lumen Fidei* 37).

We do not walk alone on this journey, but as the People of God, we as clergy and laity are interdependent, relying upon one another to transform the world. That is our call, and that is our mission.

Know Jesus Christ		Follow him		Go out
(Encounter)	⇒	(Discipleship)	⇒	(Mission)

Conclusion

Here at the end, we pull these thoughts together: Conversion of life comes from falling in love with Jesus. The love relationship that is born from encountering the living God compels us both to be and to act as Christ is and as he acts on our behalf. Preaching that fosters encounter, that builds that love relationship—that is what we have been driving toward in this retreat. In our preaching, we are not leading our people to an empty well run dry; we are leading them to living water that rises up to eternal life, an abundant life, an overflowing life, and one that satisfies as nothing else can satisfy. We begin and end with God.

Our own personal encounter and relationship with Jesus is key. We know we cannot do this ministry by ourselves; we beg the Holy Spirit to enflame our preaching. We cannot wrench people by the arm and say, "Go show and tell how wonderful the Lord is," unless they also know that wonder and have met the Lord and experienced that joy for themselves. When that happens, their jubilation will be unstoppable. That is our hope.

Are we ever done learning to preach? Fr. Greg Heille, OP, offers this:

> Learning to preach takes more effort than attending a few weekend workshops or a course at school. The preaching life is a practice, a way of life, and a way of discipleship. It is a whole person commitment, and there is simply no way to learn it or to do it or to master it. The authentic preaching life is a labor of love and a lifelong commitment.[12]

Why are we willing to make this lifelong commitment? Because we are part of a mission that is bigger than ourselves. That is our faith.

God has a mission—to be a gift of self-sacrificing love to this world. Do we *have* to have a part in that mission? No. God could have done all of this by himself. But he condescends to rely on our human words, asking us to be a part of this. We are invited to be collaborators in God's own mission. That should get us excited and make us fall in love even more and hunger to renew our own faith lives. We as preachers want to do as Jesus did. His purpose becomes our purpose. Our mission arises from his mission. We follow Jesus, and through that following, we proclaim the Good News, change the world, and bring about the kingdom of God. What could be more rewarding than that? "The joy of evangelizing always arises from grateful remembrance. . . . The apostles never forgot the moment when Jesus touched their hearts" (*Evangelii Gaudium* 13). Neither can we forget. That is our love. As *Evangelii Gaudium* teaches us,

Every Christian is a missionary to the extent that he or she has *encountered the love of God in Christ Jesus*: we no longer say that we are "disciples" and "missionaries," but rather that we are always "missionary disciples." If we are not convinced, let us look at those first disciples, who, immediately after encountering the gaze of Jesus, went forth to proclaim him joyfully: "We have found the Messiah!" (Jn 1:41). The Samaritan woman became a missionary immediately after speaking with Jesus and many Samaritans come to believe in him "because of the woman's testimony" (Jn 4:39). So too, Saint Paul, after his encounter with Jesus Christ, "immediately proclaimed Jesus" (Acts 9:20; cf. 22:6–21). So what are we waiting for? (120)

Go out and tell the Good News!

Discuss and Reflect

1. Before reading this chapter, would you say that you had preached to move disciples into missionary action? If yes, how? What does that mean to you?

2. Recall a time when your preaching moved someone to action for the good, or a time when you yourself heard preaching that moved you to action. What was it about the preaching that stimulated action? What sorts of preaching styles or strategies can help to make this happen?

3. If you could change the culture of your parish community, workplace, family, school, or other institution, what change would you bring about? What steps can you take to move in that direction? What obstacles or resistance do you note?

Try This!

St. Augustine tells us to teach, delight, and persuade—move the mind, the heart, and the will. Often the toughest dilemma is how to *move the will*: how do we spur people to *act*? Folks in all disciplines, from parenting to marketing, teaching, and preaching, wonder about that same question. In the last twenty years, there has been much study on persuasion. What of that research would be most helpful to us in preaching?

- *To persuade, speak to the heart.* Get people to care. Emotion leads to action. Though we see ourselves as rational people, we are rarely motivated by logical argument or abstract ideas alone. Preach to the heart. Also, to persuade, awaken the imagination. As you use concrete, significant detail, metaphors, and images in your preaching, those mental pictures stick. They will continue to work in people's imagination long after you preach. Offer a vision of what is possible and then ask them to act. People don't really *know* something until they have done something with it.

- *To persuade, there is nothing as effective as story.* The Christian meta-narrative has motivated people to act for two thousand years. Particular kinds of stories give people *the courage* to act, others show people *how* to act, and still others give listeners the *energy* or inspiration to act. Use stories purposefully, not simply to entertain but to inspire to action. As you work on the function of your homily, determine *how* you want to move your people. Study the chart of plot types on the next page and pick one for your upcoming homily. Use them often to move your people toward mission.[13]

Once you know what to listen for in these three types of stories, you'll begin to hear snippets of local stories all around you. Do you have Good Samaritans, Mother Teresas, underdogs, or sinners-to-saints in your own parish and in your own town? Preach their stories to get others to act—with courage, to do likewise, and/or to be energized by innovative solutions. Share that homily with others and tell how your people responded with action.

Type of Story to Preach	In Your Homily, Ask for a Response
Challenge Plot We get the courage to act from a story of challenge. *Classic examples* • The underdog story • The triumph over adversity story • The sinner-to-saint story *What it does* • Inspires by appealing to our best selves • Stirs our courage • Makes us want to work harder, take on new challenges, and overcome obstacles **Connection Plot** We want to be a better person because a stellar example shows us how to act. *Classic examples* • The mercy of the Good Samaritan • The forgiveness of the father in the parable of the prodigal son • The video "To Not At" *What it does* • Motivates by showing how personal care and concern can bridge a gap between people • Energizes by identification: "If this person can do that, so can I." • Mends a relationship or solves a problem in a personal kind of way	Try presenting an unmet need or local obstacle. Invite your community to respond with resolution and bravery, either individually or collectively, or both. With a challenge plot, conclude with an appeal to courage and commitment. Point out difficulties in relationships in everyday daily life. Where do we struggle in our interactions with other people? Following the example in the story, suggest doing something concrete to fix that relational gap, strain, or brokenness (and then perhaps report back in some way). With a connection plot, conclude with an appeal to "go and do likewise."
Creativity Plot Stories with a twist are mentally stimulating. That wakes us up to new possibilities, giving us energy to act. *Classic examples* • Feeding of the five thousand. Problem: we're hungry; standard response: go buy something to eat; clever response: take what you have and multiply them. • Mother Teresa. To the overwhelming problem of the poverty on the streets of Calcutta: pick up one, just one. *What it does* • Awakens the mind; wrestles to solve an age-old puzzle • Approaches difficulty in an inventive way • Illustrates that a well-understood problem with a standard response doesn't work–until someone finds a new solution.	Ask them to imagine new solutions to old problems in the difficulties of the world in which they live. Ask, "What can you and I do here, now, to solve these difficulties?" Stimulate their creativity. Don't let them be passive recipients of your homiletic message. With a creativity plot, conclude by inviting your people into a new way of seeing and living their individual and communal lives.

Read or View

Read or view additional materials found in this companion folder: https://bit.ly/RememberingWhyWePreach or use this code:

The materials for this chapter include the following:

Sample homily by Fr. William J. Bausch, "The Janitor's Hands," in *The Word In and Out of Season: Homilies for Preachers*, 112–16 (Mystic, CT: Twenty-Third Publications, 2000).

Jack Jezreel, "A Baptismal Faith that Does Justice," chap. 7 in *What We Have Seen and Heard: Fostering Baptismal Witness in the World*, ed. Michael E. Connors, 93–100 (Eugene, OR: Wipf and Stock, 2017). All materials used with permission.

Suggested Reading for Further Study

Allen, O. Wesley, Jr. *Preaching in the Era of Trump*. St. Louis, MO: Chalice Press, 2017.

- In spite of the provocative title, chapter 6, "Making the Church Great Again," speaks clearly to preaching to inspire mission within today's world.

Heath, Chip, and Dan Heath. *Made to Stick: Why Some Ideas Survive and Others Die*. New York: Random House, 2007.

- This book is a beneficial read in learning to communicate ideas in ways that are memorable or "sticky." Chapter 6, "Stories," further clarifies the use of plot and narrative in creating communications that are persuasive and unforgettable.

Appendix 1

Group Meeting Suggested Outline

Preparation for the Meeting

- Check that all electronics are working; homily viewing can be slowed by technical mishaps.

- Read the summary pages for the upcoming unit.

- Determine which videos will be viewed at least a week ahead of the meeting so you can prepare. Share the link to the videos that will be viewed.

- Write down your responses to the discussion questions for the unit that you have been implementing this month. Bring those written thoughts with you to the group discussion.

Meal Together Before or After (Optional, but Encouraged)

Opening Prayer

Check-In (30 Minutes)

- *Personal check-in* (15 minutes): What is the weather like in your soul today? How is it going (and so on)? And/or a spiritual growth check-in: Here is how I experience God, the questions that I have been asking, and so forth.

- *Homily implementation check-in* (15 minutes or more): Discussion of last (month's) topic:
  - » How did you implement the unit readings in your preaching this past month? What went well? Where would you like to continue to grow?
  - » How did the "Try This" exercise go for you? From the readings, what captured your imagination?

First Homily Evaluation (30 Minutes)

Have each homilist lead the discussion of his preaching. First, give context and any learning goals the preacher is working on. Then the other members of the group can give listener feedback. Each member speaks to the following question: how did this homily affect me/help me to encounter God? Give one strength and one area for growth.

Prayer for the First Preacher and His Parish (5 Minutes)

Second Homily Evaluation (30 Minutes)

This follows the same procedure as the First Homily Evaluation.

Prayer for the Second Preacher and His Parish (5 Minutes)

Moving Forward (30 Minutes)

Taking Ownership
- From the material offered for the upcoming month, what concrete "try this" suggestions shall we work on?
- What further reading do we agree to tackle as a group?

Lectio

Prayerfully read the upcoming Sunday's readings and identify preliminary thoughts. Bring your congregation with you as you read. Note a word or thought that speaks to you: scribble on the paper, and share with the group your thoughts, imagination, and discernment.

Closing/Intercessory Prayer (5-10 Minutes)

Share what to pray for each other in the upcoming month—at least one prayer request each.

Appendix 2

Homily Feedback Form

Homilist's name _____

Evaluator's name _____

Date _____

Following each writing prompt, please offer your comments as a listener of this homily.

1. Encounter: Pulling all of the elements below together, this homily evoked in me an encounter with the living God; it brought me into a closer relationship with one of the persons of the Holy Trinity.

2. One Point: The homily had a clear unity/coherence. This is the Good News about God that I heard:

The focus and function I heard were these:

3. Personal: In listening to this homily, I heard a man/woman of God speaking. The preacher's own relationship with God and journey of faith gave glory to God as the source of her/his life and strength.

4. Delivery: The homily demonstrated effective communication skills in pace, tone, vocal inflection, volume, intensity, pause, vowel length, facial expression, gesture, and body. The homilist's delivery was sincere, authentic, appropriately personal, and engaging.

5. Form/Structure: The homily had a clear progression of thoughts and was easy to follow. It had an engaging opening, a sensible structure/form that maintained focus and developed interest, effective transitions, and a memorable closing.

6. Scripture: The interpretation of the scriptural text was exegetically sound, easily grasped, and functioned as a lens through which to interpret our lives today.

7. Listener Orientation: The homily evinced a sound understanding of the audience, culture, and context; the homily spoke to the people gathered for this specific occasion.

8. Left Brain/Cognition: The homily clarified something for me; the homily was theologically rich and preached something urgent and important to our faith. It had intellectual substance and invited me to further reflection.

9. Right Brain/Imagination: The homily awakened my imagination in a way that invited me to transformation, to see God, myself, and/or the world with new eyes; the homilist made effective use of story, image, and metaphor.

10. Heart: The homily touched my heart deeply and stirred passion; it invited me to fall in love with Jesus.

11. Will: The homily persuaded me to want to do or be something more.

12. Liturgical: The homily was appropriately embedded in the liturgy; it nurtured thanksgiving and worship at the eucharistic table, and a sense of mission or service to others in daily life.

13. Stickiness: I will remember this homily and share its content and images with others.

Additional Comments

Appendix 3

Personal Goal-Setting Sheet

Setting goals focuses your learning. If you are working with others, it helps them to focus their feedback on how you wish to grow in your preaching. After analyzing your preaching or working with a coach, determine two goals that you will commit yourself to during this preaching retreat process. Aim high but not so high that your goals are unreachable. Remember you are striving to create a genuine opportunity for authentic encounter in preaching. What two steps can you take that will help you to get there? Consider setting one delivery goal and one structure/content goal or a structure and a content goal.

GOAL 1	GOAL 2
*****	*****
How will I know when I have accomplished it?	How will I know when I have accomplished it?

Appendix 4
Peer Group Gathering Schedule

If you are going to form a peer learning group, below is a chart for you to record all of your pertinent information.

Gathering	Location	Time	Viewing Which Videos? (Name homilist and homily)
1			
2			
3			
4			
5			
6			
7			
8			

Notes

Introduction

1. See Karla Bellinger, *Connecting Pulpit and Pew: Breaking Open the Conversation about Catholic Preaching* (Collegeville, MN: Liturgical Press, 2014), 90–91.

2. Bishops' Committee on Priestly Life and Ministry, *Fulfilled in Your Hearing: The Homily in the Sunday Assembly* (Washington, DC: US Conference of Catholic Bishops, 1982), 21. Emphasis ours.

1. Help Them Find God

1. The "Try This" exercise for this month suggests a spiritual reading list on pages   . Be attentive to how the holy ones expressed their experience of God.

2. Suggestions for spiritual reading from some of our personal favorites are in "Read or View" section. Share other personal favorites with each other as well.

2. Preaching the Paschal Mystery

1. See Kendra Creasy Dean, *Almost Christian: What the Faith of Our Teenagers Is Telling the American Church* (New York: Oxford University Press, 2010), for a richer explication of that mindset.

2. Bishops' Committee on Clergy, Consecrated Life, and Vocations, *Preaching the Mystery of Faith: The Sunday Homily* (Washington, DC: US Conference of Catholic Bishops, 2012), 15.

3. *Fulfilled in Your Hearing*, 23.

4. Peter John Cameron, *Why Preach? Encountering Christ in God's Word* (San Francisco: Ignatius Press, 2009), 48.

5. Mary Alice Mulligan et al., *Believing in Preaching: What Listeners Hear in Sermons* (St. Louis, MO: Chalice Press, 2005), 13.

6. See Peter John Cameron, "Homiletic Missteps: The Poison of Moralism and Its Antidote," chap. 5 in *Why Preach?* 125–27.

7. Paul Janowiak, *The Holy Preaching: The Sacramentality of the Word in the Liturgical Assembly* (Collegeville, MN: Liturgical Press, 2000). See especially chapter 5, "The Holy Preaching: A Sacramentality of the Word as 'Fulfilled in Our Hearing.'"

8. Mary Catherine Hilkert, *Naming Grace: Preaching and the Sacramental Imagination* (New York: Continuum, 1998), 49.

9. For endless preaching possibilities, see the chart in the "Try This" section on page 24.

10. *Preaching the Mystery of Faith*, 17.
11. Cameron, *Why Preach?* 52.

3. Preaching as a Spiritual Practice

1. Dag Hammarskjöld, *Markings* (New York: Vintage Books, 2006).
2. Sally A. Brown and Luke A. Powery, *Ways of the Word: Learning to Preach for Your Time and Place* (Minneapolis: Fortress Press, 2016), 58.
3. Bellinger, *Connecting Pulpit and Pew*, 71.
4. Anna Carter Florence, *Preaching as Testimony* (Louisville, KY: Westminster John Knox Press, 2007), 113.
5. For more on Ignatius's thought on contemplation in action, see the fourteenth chapter of James Martin, *The Jesuit Guide to (Almost) Everything* (New York: HarperCollins, 2010).
6. Stephen Vincent DeLeers, *Written Text Becomes Living Word: The Vision and Practice of Sunday Preaching* (Collegeville, MN: Liturgical Press, 2004), 179.
7. Karl Rahner said similarly, "The Christian of the future will be a mystic or he will not exist at all." *Theological Investigations*, vol. 20, *Concern for the Church* (New York: Herder & Herder, 1981), 149.
8. See Deborah Wilhelm's presentation at the 2017 Notre Dame preaching conference "'Murder Your Darlings': How to Edit Words for Effective Preaching," July 25, 2017, posted on YouTube, September 1, 2017, https://youtu.be/JrDih11ufZg. Text of this presentation can be found in Michael E. Connors, ed., *Effective Preaching: Bringing People into an Encounter with God* (Chicago: Liturgy Training Publications, 2019), 111–22.
9. *Fulfilled in Your Hearing*, 8.

4. Preaching as a Pastoral Practice

1. *Fulfilled in Your Hearing*, 4.
2. "The Church: Community of the New Evangelization," United States Conference of Catholic Bishops, accessed May 9, 2022, https://www.usccb.org.
3. We will expand on this idea as we conclude this book with a chapter on "Preaching to Move Disciples into Mission."
4. For contrast, watch an old movie from the 1940s or 1950s and see how slowly each scene unfolds.
5. See Bellinger, "Surrounded by the Greats of History," chap. 4 in *Connecting Pulpit and Pew*, for a robust discussion of how preaching has adapted through the centuries as a response to changes in culture.
6. Karla J. Bellinger, "Are You Talking to Me? A Study of Young Listeners' Connection with Catholic Sunday Preaching" (DMin diss., Aquinas Institute, St. Louis, MO, 2012).

7. In an airplane conversation with an executive vice president from a Georgia college, she related how surprised her administration was about the survey results from their students: the students did not ask for more online courses; they consistently preferred face-to-face interaction with a teacher.

5. Preaching as Spiritual Leadership

1. "Pope Francis: Priests Should Be 'Shepherds Living with the Smell of the Sheep,'" *Catholic Telegraph*, March 28, 2013, http://www.thecatholictelegraph.com.

2. *Preaching the Mystery of Faith*, 31.

3. Mary Alice Mulligan and Ronald J. Allen, *Make the Word Come Alive: Lessons from the Laity* (St. Louis, MO: Chalice Press, 2005). This is book 3 of the four-part series *Channels of Listening*.

4. In "The Holy Spirit and the Mysticism of Everyday Life," in *The Content of Faith: The Best of Karl Rahner's Theological Writings*, ed. Karl Lehmann and Albert Raffelt, 367–72 (New York: Crossroad, 2014), see a robust list of Holy Spirit experiences that may be on the edge of consciousness, the naming of which would greatly add to the depth of a homily.

5. *Fulfilled in Your Hearing*, 7.

6. Thomas G. Long, *The Witness of Preaching*, 3rd ed. (Louisville, KY: Westminster John Knox Press, 2016), 111–12.

7. Long, *Witness of Preaching*, 114–15.

8. Fred B. Craddock, *Preaching* (Nashville: Abingdon, 1985), 85.

9. Long, *Witness of Preaching*, 143.

10. Craddock, *Preaching*, 172–74.

11. In *Made to Stick* by Chip and Dan Heath (New York: Random House, 2007), the authors describe the "Curse of Knowledge": the observation that most of us are not aware that what we understand in our head is not the same as what is going on in another person's head. They use the two-person tapping game, "Name That Tune," to illustrate this concept.

12. *The Story of God with Morgan Freeman*, National Geographic, 2016–2019, https://www.nationalgeographic.com.

6. Opening the Conversation between Pulpit and Pew

1. David Shea, "Unmet Needs in Catholic Preaching: A Project of the Archdiocese of Cincinnati," *Seminary Journal* 16 (2010): 33.

2. A helpful look at preaching feedback is found in chapter 19 of Ken Untener's *Preaching Better: Practical Suggestions for Homilists* (New York: Paulist Press, 1999), discussed later in this chapter.

3. Craddock, *Preaching*, 182.

4. Untener calls his method of homiletic detective work "Columbo-style" (*Preaching Better*, 1). These thousands of comments became the impetus for his book *Preaching Better*.

5. For more on this topic, see Bellinger, *Connecting Pulpit and Pew*, chapter 8 for the "why" and chapter 9 for the "how" of initiating parish conversation on preaching. Consider the power dynamics of your parish structure carefully. Would you be able to volunteer to your bishop or superior that his homily is boring, too academic, or meandering? Would you be more likely to give that input if he first asked for it?

6. *Fulfilled in Your Hearing*, 36–38.

7. Other suggestions for study, depending on the reading level of your participants, might be *Connecting Pulpit and Pew* by Bellinger and *Preaching Better* by Untener.

8. Douglas Stone and Sheila Heen, "Dismantle Distortions," chap. 8 in *Thanks for the Feedback: The Science and Art of Receiving Feedback Well*, 165–82 (New York: Viking, 2014).

9. Stone and Heen, "Cultivate a Growth Identity," chap. 9 in *Thanks for the Feedback*, 183–206, 193; the authors suggest cultivating an identity in which we see ourselves as people who can continually grow.

10. Untener, *Preaching Better*, 1.

11. Bellinger, *Connecting Pulpit and Pew*, 145.

7. Moving through Encounter to Discipleship

1. "The Concluding Document of the Fifth General Conference of the Bishops of Latin America and the Caribbean," 18, Shrine of Aparecida, Brazil, May 13, 2007, https://www. celam.org/aparecida/Ingles.pdf.

2. Francis, *The Joy of Discipleship: Reflections from Pope Francis on Walking with Christ* (Chicago: Loyola Press, 2016), 35. Italics in the original.

3. Dietrich Bonhoeffer, *The Cost of Discipleship* (New York: Touchstone, 1995; originally published in German, 1937), 63.

4. See an expansion of these facets in Kathleen A. Cahalan's "The Call and Practice of Discipleship," in *Introducing the Practice of Ministry*, 1–23 (Collegeville, MN: Liturgical Press, 2010).

5. Quoted in Sherry A. Weddell, *Forming Intentional Disciples: The Path to Knowing and Following Jesus* (Huntington, IN: Our Sunday Visitor, 2012), 223.

6. David Buttrick says to handle the contrapuntal carefully, but do not ignore the oppositions to the Gospel, even if only for a few sentences or a short paragraph within one of your moves; that way you have acknowledged that there are potential resistances and you can defuse them. See *Homiletic: Moves and Structures* (Minneapolis: Fortress Press, 1987), 30–32.

7. At the same time, they are hungry to talk about finding meaning and purpose in the activities of everyday life. To dig deeper into this phenomenon, see David Lose, "Do You Feel Called?" Day1, September 5, 2014, https://day1.org.

8. Christian Smith, *Soul Searching: The Religious and Spiritual Lives of American Teenagers* (New York: Oxford University Press, 2005), 162–71.

9. Bellinger, *Connecting Pulpit and Pew*, 93.

10. Jeremy Driscoll, "Preaching the Resurrection: Central Content of the New Evangelization," in *To All the World: Preaching and the New Evangelization*, ed. Michael E. Connors, 139–53 (Collegeville, MN: Liturgical Press, 2016), 143.

11. Pope Francis, "Pope: True Christians and Cheerful Faces and Eyes Full of Joy," homily for February 18, 2017, Vatican Radio, http://www.archivioradiovaticana.va.

12. Damian J. Ference, "Why Vocational Programs Don't Work," *Homiletic and Pastoral Review*, February 1, 2011, http://www.hprweb.com.

13. William E. Simon Jr., *Great Catholic Parishes: A Living Mosaic* (Notre Dame, IN: Ave Maria Press, 2016), 59.

14. Bonhoeffer, *Cost of Discipleship*.

8. Preaching to Move Disciples into Mission

1. For further reading on this, see Stephen Bevans, "From 'Missions' to 'Mission': Trinity, World Christianity, and Baptismal Witness," in *"What We Have Seen and Heard": Fostering Baptismal Witness in the World*, ed. Michael E. Connors, 74–88 (Eugene, OR: Pickwick Publications, 2017). See also Bevans's address of the same name at the University of Notre Dame, June 23, 2015, posted on YouTube, October 16, 2015, https://youtu.be/PJpyEIOv-Ro.

2. This message was reiterated and extended in *Apostolicam Actuositatem* (*The Decree on the Apostolate of Lay People*; 1965). For instance, *AA* 2 says, "The Christian vocation is, of its nature, a vocation to the apostolate as well." *AA* 9 states that "the lay apostolate, in all its many aspects, is exercised both in the church and in the world."

3. Attributed to Ernest T. Campbell of Riverside Church in New York City, who quoted it in a sermon in 1970 and published it as "Give Ye Them to Eat" in 1973 (Internet Archive, January 25, 1970, https://archive.org/details/sermongiveyethem00camp). On the internet, it is often (mis-)attributed to Mark Twain.

4. Francis, "Angelus," Saint Peter's Square, January 6, 2014, https://www.vatican.va.

5. Sally A. Brown, *Sunday's Sermon for Monday's World: Preaching to Shape Daring Witness* (Grand Rapids, MI: Eerdmans, 2020).

6. Robin Gomes, "Pope Urges Nurses to Touch the Sick Like Jesus," *Vatican News*, March 3, 2018, http://www.vaticannews.va.

7. For a popular best seller on this topic, see Rick Warren, *The Purpose Driven Life: What on Earth Am I Here For?* (Grand Rapids, MI: Zondervan, 2013).

8. An example for further reading would be Pontifical Council for Justice and Peace, *Vocation of the Business Leader: A Reflection* (Vatican City: Dicastery for Promoting Integral Human Development, 2012).

9. James Mallon, *Divine Renovation: Bringing Your Parish from Maintenance to Mission* (New London, CT: Twenty-Third Publications, 2014), 257.

10. Gregory Heille, *The Preaching of Pope Francis: Missionary Discipleship and the Ministry of the Word* (Collegeville, MN: Liturgical Press, 2015), xi.

11. These three types of story are summarized from Chip Heath and Dan Heath, *Made to Stick: Why Some Ideas Survive and Others Die* (New York: Random House, 2007), 228–31.

Karla J. Bellinger is a Catholic speaker and the founding executive director of the Institute for Homiletics at the University of Dallas. She previously served as the associate director of the John S. Marten Program in Homiletics and Liturgics at the University of Notre Dame, where she also was a member of the theology department faculty.

Bellinger earned a bachelor of science degree from North Carolina State University, a master of arts in theology from the University of Notre Dame, and a doctorate of ministry in preaching from the Aquinas Institute. She is president of the Catholic Association of Teachers of Homiletics and is a member of the Academy of Homiletics, and the North American Academy of Liturgy. Bellinger is certified as a lay ecclesial minister and a master catechist. She is also a master gardener.

She is author of *Connecting Pulpit and Pew* and *Living the Word* and has contributed to several other books. Her work has appeared in *Homiletics, The Deacon, Catechetical Leader, Momentum,* and *Seminary Journal.*

Bellinger lives with her family in southwestern Michigan.

instituteforhomiletics.org

Fr. Michael E. Connors, CSC, is director of the John S. Marten Program in Homiletics and Liturgics, as well as a faculty member in the Department of Theology at the University of Notre Dame. He was ordained a priest of the Congregation of Holy Cross in 1984.

Connors earned a bachelor's degree from Illinois College, a master of divinity degree from Notre Dame, and a doctor of theology from Regis College at the Toronto School of Theology. He is a past president of the Catholic Association of Teachers of Homiletics and a member of the Academy of Homiletics, the Catholic Theological Society of America, and the College Theology Society. Connors is the editor of five books on homiletics, and the author of two monographs, including *Preaching for Discipleship: Preparing Homilies for Christian Initiation* and *Inculturated Pastoral Planning: The US Hispanic Experience.*

https://theology.nd.edu/graduate-programs/initiatives/marten-program/

AVE

Ave Maria Press

Founded in 1865, Ave Maria Press,
a ministry of the Congregation of
Holy Cross, is a Catholic publishing
company that serves the spiritual and
formative needs of the Church and its
schools, institutions, and ministers;
Christian individuals and families; and
others seeking spiritual nourishment.

For a complete listing of titles from

Ave Maria Press

Sorin Books

Forest of Peace

Christian Classics

visit www.avemariapress.com

Ave Maria Press
Notre Dame, IN
A Ministry of the United States Province of Holy Cross